HOW TO WRITE A NONFICTION BOOK IN 24 HOURS

A SIMPLE STEP-BY-STEP SYSTEM FOR WRITING A GOOD BOOK FAST

DALE L. ROBERTS

How to Write a Nonfiction Book in 24 Hours: A Simple Step-by-Step System for Writing a Good Book Fast

All rights reserved.
Copyright ©2024 One Jacked Monkey, LLC

eBook ISBN: 978-1-63925-051-6
Paperback ISBN: 978-1-63925-052-3
Hardcover ISBN: 978-1-63925-053-0
Audiobook ISBN: 978-1-63925-054-7

All rights reserved. No part of this book may be reproduced in any form by any electronic or mechanical means, including information storage and retrieval systems, without permission in writing from the copyright owner, except by a reviewer who may quote brief passages in a review.

Some recommended links in this book are part of affiliate programs. If you purchase a product through one of the links, then I get a portion of each sale. It doesn't affect your cost and greatly helps support the cause. If you have any reservations about buying a product through my affiliate link, then Google a direct link and bypass the affiliate link.

CONTENTS

INTRODUCTION: WRITING A NONFICTION BOOK IN 24 HOURS 1

CHAPTER 1: UNDERSTANDING THE NONFICTION WRITING PROCESS 5

CHAPTER 2: SPEED TYPING TECHNIQUES FOR RAPID WRITING 15

CHAPTER 3: VOICE DICTATION FOR EFFICIENT WRITING 24

CHAPTER 4: TRANSCRIBING METHODS FOR FAST CONTENT GENERATION..... 32

CHAPTER 5: OVERCOMING TIME CONSTRAINTS AND
INCREASING WRITING EFFICIENCY 40

CHAPTER 6: MOTIVATION AND CONFIDENCE IN COMPLETING
A NONFICTION BOOK... 51

CHAPTER 7: POLISHING YOUR MANUSCRIPT FOR PUBLISHING 60

CHAPTER 8: PUBLISHING OPTIONS 69

CHAPTER 9: MARKETING AND PROMOTING YOUR BOOK 78

CONCLUSION: ACHIEVING YOUR NONFICTION WRITING
GOALS IN LIMITED TIME 88

A SMALL ASK... 93

ABOUT THE AUTHOR 94
SPECIAL THANKS 95
RESOURCES... 96
REFERENCES 99

GET MY BESTSELLER BOOK LAUNCH CHECKLIST ABSOLUTELY FREE!

Want to launch your book to bestseller status on Amazon? Sign up for my email newsletter today and get my **Bestseller Book Launch Checklist** for FREE! This step-by-step plan will help you make your book a hit.

But that's not all! When you subscribe, you'll also get my email newsletter packed with the latest self-publishing news and tips. Get all you need to know in just one or two emails per week.

Subscribe now and grab your free checklist at DaleLinks.com/Checklist

Win **awards** and get **reviews** for **your book**

25% off your first purchase

bookawardpro.com

"I've used dozens of book cover design services over the last ten years, and none compare to the level of quality and professionalism that Miblart delivers."

— *Dale L. Roberts*

Miblart - a book cover design company for self-published authors

Designers who specialize in different genres	Unlimited number of revisions
No deposit to get started	You can pay in installments

GET A BOOK COVER THAT WILL BECOME YOUR N°1 MARKETING TOOL

Excellent

★★★★★ 4.9

Write a Nonfiction Book in 24 Hours

Meet **Dibbly Create.**

Your All-in-1 A.I. companion for writing, publishing & marketing your book.

With Dibbly, it's done.

Yes,
I Need Help Writing my Book

A.I. Assisted:

- ✓ Market Research
- ✓ Competitive Insights
- ✓ Amazon & Google Research
- ✓ Book Outlines
- ✓ Content-Writer
- ✓ Editing & Rewriting
- ✓ Formatting & Publish-Ready
- ✓ Much More

Try for Free!

Scan the QR Code or visit

Next level tools to help you grow.

Whether you're an aspiring author or international bestseller, we've got the tools to help you publish faster, distribute wider and manage your business easier.

Learn more by going to **d2d.tips/dale** and read on to discover some of what sets D2D apart:

- ✓ **Automated end-matter**
- ✓ **New Release Notifications for readers**
- ✓ **Payment Splitting for contributors**
- ✓ **Scheduled price changes**
- ✓ **Smashwords store coupons**
- ✓ **Universal Book Links via Books2Read.com**

 ## It's print-on-demand reimagined.

Create a paperback on draft2digital.com from your existing ebook with just a few clicks, and **create a full, wrap-around book cover from your ebook cover**. It really is that easy!

 ## THE indie bookstore.

Massive annual sales, self-serve promotion tools, and the **industry's best royalty rates** of up to 80% list. Readers love discovering breakout indie authors at smashwords.com.

INTRODUCTION: WRITING A NONFICTION BOOK IN 24 HOURS

The first time I wrote a book in under twenty-four hours was on June 27, 2020. I produced the first draft of my five-time award-winning book, *Amazon Keywords for Books*, in a little over eleven hours in front of a live audience on YouTube. That book won five book awards, earned nine additional book awards as part of an omnibus, and garnered massive attention in the indie author community, with some touting it as the "keywords bible."

Prior to that challenge, I'd written books in a month, a week, and even in a couple of days; but doing it in just one day seemed like a tall ask. At that point, I'd already been in the business of writing and publishing books for six years and had published over fifty nonfiction books in the health and fitness space. In my first year, I wrote an essay called *How to Write a Book in 48 Hours* that explained all the things an author needs to know to write quality books efficiently, so I was already familiar with what I needed to do.

Writing a book in twenty-four hours is a tall feat that comes with a lot of pressure, especially when you've never done it before. Back in 2013 when I set out to write my first book, I couldn't have fathomed doing it.

Back then, I merely put words on a virtual page, never filtering what I thought about before typing. Over a year later, I finally published a 44,000-word manuscript called *The 3 Keys to Health & Happiness: Unlock Your Greater Life*. Despite all my best efforts, that book was hammered garbage.

If only I had been given a blueprint to efficiently write and produce a quality manuscript, I could've avoided a lot of headaches, hassle, and embarrassment.

My good friend Rob Archangel once said in an interview, "Your first book is your worst book." I had that down pat because I wrote a truly awful book. Did it make some sales? Absolutely! Were those readers highly dissatisfied and leaving negative reviews? No. But it didn't stay long on the virtual shelves.

Within a few months of publishing my book, I realized that writing a good book isn't as simple as journaling or writing articles for the local small-town newspaper. I removed that first iteration fast after making quite a few repairs, with the much-needed help of a professional editor and an experienced cover designer.

I've since delisted my first book because it wasn't worth anyone's time. My situation would have been significantly better if I had specific instructions on what to do, how to do it, and when to do it. Maybe, just maybe, *The 3 Keys to Greater Health & Happiness* would've gotten its day in the sun, winning multiple book awards and getting praise within the fitness industry.

Without any real direction, my first book didn't see any of that success, and that's what brings us here. Not only have I written high-quality, full-length books within twenty-four hours once, but

INTRODUCTION: WRITING A NONFICTION BOOK IN 24 HOURS

I've now done it twice. You're reading my second successful attempt at writing a book in a day. I know it's rather meta to write a book in twenty-four hours about writing a book in twenty-four hours, but I did this again to prove how it can be done.

To be clear, I'm not promising you'll write the best book ever within one day; but if you follow this guide, you will get the first draft done. It's been my experience that writing the book isn't the hardest part; it's merely the first step in the life cycle of a book. Rather than dwell on the first draft of your book for the next year, why not cut down that time so you can focus on the subsequent steps in the process? Editing, proofreading, formatting, cover design, niche research, copywriting, publishing, marketing, and promoting are all much more involved, requiring your undivided attention for more time. Why make your first draft the hardest part?

I've often heard that the journey of a thousand miles begins with one step, so why take longer than you have to? Complete that first step so you can get to the next stages as efficiently as possible.

In this book, you will discover how to plan for your next nonfiction book and remove any friction from the process. Preparation is critical to the mission, and knowing what to ready yourself for and what does you no good will make all the difference. I've repeatedly heard that authors don't believe they can write a book in one day, but that's only because they haven't tried or fully prepared themselves for the effort.

Not everyone is an expert typist, so I'll share ways to improve in that area. You might even learn about a couple of alternatives that'll drive your word count faster than your fingers will ever be able to handle. Writing books isn't supposed to be you toiling behind an old-school electric typewriter, clacking key after key to make a somewhat readable manuscript. You have the freedom to choose how to write in the most efficient way that you feel is most comfortable.

That's what leads me to putting a spotlight on an area I've never covered in previous books: mindset. Don't worry, I will not go completely into the self-help genre; but I feel it's helpful to share words of wisdom and encouragement so when you hit a roadblock, you know that it's merely a speed bump on your road to victory. After all, if you can't get your mind right, how can you ever expect to pull your best efforts from it? By the time you finish this book, I'll grease your creative wheels and pump you up so you see exactly what I do and can see how you can do it, too.

I truly believe writing a book isn't the hard part; the hard part is committing to finishing it and doing all the work that comes after the first draft. Once you write it, what comes next? I'll cover exactly what you need to launch your own nonfiction book successfully—everything from editing to post-book launch promotions. The best part is this: Once you know this system, you can tweak your approach, fine tune your writing process, and do it again and again.

And, you won't have to do it in a live YouTube video, so you have far less pressure to perform. With that said, let's dive into *How to Write a Nonfiction Book in 24 Hours*!

CHAPTER 1:
UNDERSTANDING THE NONFICTION WRITING PROCESS

What should I write about? It's a simple enough question, but it is very complex for a lot of folks breaking into the business of writing and self-publishing. I don't fault those authors for not knowing what they want to write about. In fact, I had wanted to write for years but never did so because I didn't know what to write about.

That changed when a corporate wellness coach at my day job challenged me to write a book about health and fitness. I was so passionate about healthy living that she felt I could write an entire book. When presented with the challenge of writing a book about a topic I loved, I got right to work.

When asking yourself what to write about, determine what you are most passionate about. Do you have insights into a specific industry or niche? No matter how big or how small that insight might seem, do you have solutions for people? Go with the path of least resistance. Lean into what you know. People will thank you for it.

Even after landing on a topic, once I started writing, I didn't realize that I did not have a clear understanding of my ideal reader. Less than a year after releasing my debut publication, I shared it with my good friend, Mark Stafford. He looked at it and asked, "Who is this book for?"

"It's for everyone," I said.

"So, you wrote a health and fitness book that's good for teenagers *and* older adults?" he responded.

Mark stumped me. I knew deep down that the book was not suitable for both groups of people. For somebody between twenty and thirty years old with no special health conditions, sure. For everyone else, it wasn't specific enough.

That's why you need to get clear around who your audience is. When you're writing, you need to know exactly who you're speaking to. You don't talk to a teenager the same way you would speak to a senior citizen. Sure, you can communicate using some universal language. However, when it comes down to each group's specific needs, you've got to really dial that in.

Know your audience. Who is your audience? Your ideal reader, the person who will enjoy your content the most and will share it with other people. Once you understand what you're going to write about and who you'll be writing for, you'll still want to invest time in researching your niche. Prolific writer Stephen King once shared that if you want to be a writer, you must do two things: read and write a lot!

I completely understand that you might feel confident in your writing abilities, but there is always room to improve. The best way to improve is through practice and study. If you're looking to break into the self-help world, then you'd better be reading the authors who are crushing it in that niche. Understand what they say, how they communicate, and what makes their books so great that millions of people will part ways with their hard-earned dollars for a chance to read their work.

Naturally, reading other books is only one part of the process. You want to be mindful of other authors' title choices, book descriptions, covers, and one thing that can function like a cheat sheet for your book—the reviews. Reviews are like gold, especially if they come with substance. Don't merely look at the overall rating for the books you study—look at what readers are saying.

I'm naturally inclined to check out the negative reviews because they provide insights into what the author didn't deliver on. That is a potential gap in the market you can capitalize on. Now, I'm not saying to get intel from low reviews that criticize opposing political ideologies or religions; I'm referring to substantive feedback about how well the author delivered on the expectations of the reader.

For instance, if you see reviews for a nonfiction book in your niche that say the reader expected more workouts in the book, then see if you can incorporate that feedback into your fitness publication.

Look at a wide range of reviews to see where other books get it right and where they go wrong. Now you have insights into what that audience is craving.

RESEARCH & GATHER RELEVANT INFO

As you study your chosen genre, make sure you collect data and resources you find useful. They'll come in handy later when you need to lean on credible third-party resources. When I'm writing my first draft, I don't rely too heavily on research. Later on, when I do my first edits, I'll look up resources to cite in the book. Often, I'll type **"CITE SOURCE"** in all caps and bolded so it's easy to pick out in my first rounds of edits.

The most important part about finishing a first draft as efficiently as possible is saving that extra time to stop and cite your source. Yes, you should cite your source before you publish, but, no, you do not have to include it in your first draft. That can wait until you edit your book.

From a structural standpoint, you may later decide to rearrange passages, delete paragraphs, or even remove entire chapters. Can you imagine taking that extra time to find a source, cite it, and put it in your document, only to delete it later? Speak with as much authority as possible when you're writing. Sort out the rest later, because no one will see your first draft but you.

When you're gathering resources and information, you'll want to double-check all your facts to make sure they are 100% correct. This means you should not rely on Wikipedia as a source. Sorry, folks. Wikipedia is a crowd-created informational database that is flooded with misinformation and half-truths. Don't believe me? Look up a show on YouTube called *Wikipedia: Fact or Fiction*.

Whenever you find information that cites another source, track it. Don't be naïve enough to trust some random website to give factual information. A good, credible source will credit the origin of their information.

Another great way to get info is by interviewing experts in your field. An old pal and editor buddy, James Ranson, once wrote a book called *Don't Write a Crappy Book*. Then he brought together a veritable who's who panel of guests. The experts donated their time and answered questions openly. James communicated his points while referencing credible resources in his niche. Sure, he could've leaned on his own education and experience to present facts, but sharing the same views as another expert carries more weight.

When you're compiling your resources, consider keeping any print materials in an easily accessible location. For online resources, you'll want to store the web address and the title for future reference. Store a folder of bookmarks in your preferred browser and make a list in your preferred word processing program.

I have References and Resources pages at the end of my books where readers can dig deeper into what I wrote. Will every reader check these sources? Probably not; but it's an extra touch every nonfiction book should have, whether half a page or ten pages.

When you want to pull quotes from a source, note them in your manuscript. As for how much of a quote you can use, it depends. The shorter the better. If you don't have permission to use their quote—whether granted through their website or their published book—it becomes a little shaky.

According to the U.S. Copyright Office, the fair use doctrine promotes freedom of expression by permitting the unlicensed use of copyright-protected works in certain circumstances.[i] There are a whole lot of gray areas here, and this doctrine only protects you so much, especially if you're making money off somebody else's intellectual property.

Yes, people will appreciate you crediting them as the source of information, but there are a few who don't appreciate you profiting from their words. Sadly, I'm not a lawyer, nor do I play one on TV. I'll refer you to a respected industry expert, Helen Sedwick, who wrote *The Self-Publisher's Legal Handbook*. She's an experienced indie author and business attorney.

I'd recommend limiting your use of quotes in favor of writing your interpretation of what they've said. When you're leaning on resources, you don't have to let the source do all the heavy lifting. Take what you've learned and share it in your own way. Every person has their own unique voice that will resonate differently depending on the reader.

While I might be your favorite author who covers self-publishing, there are quite a few people who don't care for how I present myself and the way I communicate. My good friend and longtime supporter Anthony Fleischmann once told me,

Your vibe attracts your tribe.

I was feeling discouraged after going live on my channel a few times, only to find I lost subscribers after posting each video. Anthony shared his advice when I needed it most and helped me realize that I'm not everyone's cup of tea. Of course, I've always known that. The cool part is I trusted the process. Later, those same videos brought in new subscribers who *did* appreciate my content.

In a future chapter, we'll discuss how an editor will help sort out references and resources. To recap, in the pre-writing phase, you just want to collect all you can.

In keeping with the premise of this book, I recommend you do not include doing research in the twenty-four hours of writing time.

Research can take anywhere from weeks to months depending on how much time you can devote and the complexity of the topic.

Don't wait until the last minute to research your niche. Your desire to write a nonfiction book should come from years of reading, studying, and practicing in your area of expertise. At the very least, you should know where you can find the information you need to incorporate research into your nonfiction book.

CREATING AN OUTLINE

Next comes the part you need to pay close attention to: your outline. I applaud any author who can meticulously craft beautiful prose through discovery writing. Some people naturally write in a linear path that provides readers with a solution to their problems.

In order to stay on track to complete your book in twenty-four hours, you're going to need an almost paint-by-numbers approach to be on the safe side. This means you'll want to organize your ideas so you know precisely where you're going and why.

The first step in outlining a book is to go back to your ideal reader. Ask the common questions plaguing the reader in your niche. Then, write all the concepts you feel best solve that reader's problem. Once you have a page or two of talking points, organize them in a way that makes the most sense. You'll want to take the reader on a journey, so put your talking points in a clear and easy-to-follow order. If it helps, consider what would work best in a conversation or on-stage presentation and organize your outline the same way you would structure a natural conversation.

Nonfiction authors have an advantage over fiction authors. Since we provide a solution to the reader's problem, we can easily create the outline for a book simply by putting together a table of contents. Chapter titles should reveal exactly what a reader can expect, or at the very least, entice the reader to read more. Do you need to be a copywriting expert to craft interesting titles for your chapters? No, but it certainly helps if you think of your chapter titles as ways to:

- Optimize your content for search engines
- Entice readers to read your book

How you develop chapter titles is completely up to you. Worst-case scenario, take the simple approach. A prime example of keeping it simple is what TV shows like *It's Always Sunny in Philadelphia* do. Each episode tells the viewers exactly what the story will be about:

- "The Gang Goes Bowling"
- "Charlie Rules the World"
- "Frank's Back in Business"

They cater to their audience by being direct about the content of each episode. You should think of your future book the same way. Label the chapters so you know what is best to write for each section.

Under each chapter, organize similar thoughts and ideas so readers get the full idea of what you're sharing. For instance, in my book about getting reviews, I separated the concepts of editorial reviews and advance reader copy (ARC) reviews. Each topic needs a separate explanation and involves slightly different approaches, so I wouldn't want to put them in the same chapter if I could help it. If I'm talking about the top tools for forming an ARC team, I would include that in the chapter about advance reader reviews.

The same would go for editorial reviews. Should I want to share credible resources for getting editorial reviews, I would keep that separate from the section on advance reader reviews.

Properly arranging an organized outline can be key to finishing your book in a timely manner. A well-structured outline helps you to write seamlessly from one chapter to the next, so you will never wonder if you have covered a point or will cover a point. You might decide to reference future chapters where readers can expect more content. Having that outline will help you predict that section and share where it'll be. Again, you can always rearrange and sort your first draft during editing. If something seems a bit out of place, don't force it too much. Keep writing and resolve the problem during the editing process.

When you uncover a point that requires a deeper explanation, break down your outline into relevant subtopics until the reader has a clearer understanding of what you're saying.

For instance, if I were to write a chapter about push-ups, it could look something like this:

1. Push-Ups

    A. Why are they good for you?
    B. What benefits do you get from them?
    C. How do you perform push-ups?

        a. Are there modifications?

    b. What precautions should you take and what actions should you avoid while doing push-ups?
    c. What are frequent questions about push-ups?
    d. What are some common mistakes with push-ups?

Granted, that's a very crude breakdown, but it still paints a picture of what you'll want to do when outlining your book. You can be as brief or as detailed as you want. I simply need a small cue, and I'll take off from there. It'll take a little trial and error to find out what outlining strategy works best for you.

Having an outline will give you a greater advantage when writing a book in twenty-four hours compared to not having one. Don't sweat it too much if you deviate occasionally from that outline. When you do, simply adjust your content accordingly. It's possible that you may realize a point you're trying to make isn't necessary until a later chapter. In that case, move the content to where it needs to go. You can handle that in the edits, but if you can fix the outline as you go, it'll make the work easier when you edit what you've written later on.

CHAPTER 2:
SPEED TYPING TECHNIQUES FOR RAPID WRITING

I was a freshman in high school when I enrolled in Mrs. Nagel's typing class. In the back of my mind, I thought it'd be an easy A and a better alternative than classes I had zero interest in, like shop. I already knew by then that I wanted to grow up to be a writer, but I'd convinced myself that my handwriting was perfectly adequate for writing first drafts.

I'm not the biggest advocate of handwriting these days since I'm much more proficient at typing now. Back then I wasn't a fan of typing. In fact, as the entire class hammered away on loud electronic typewriters, I was as bored as if I were watching paint dry.

Clunk, clunk...clunk, clunk, clunk...ching!

During the first few weeks of class, we had to follow along to the rhythm of Mrs. Nagel's alphabet soup.

"F, space, K, space, F, space..." She gasped for air. "...K, space, F, space."

This went on for an eternity, and I hated it. I didn't really see what she was getting at, or if the lessons were really working. I took an entire semester with her, easily three to four months, and I aced the class.

Thankfully, technology has advanced so much since 1990 that you don't have to rely on overpowered, antiquated pieces of equipment like a Smith Corona typewriter. By the time I graduated in 1994, my school had a computer lab stocked with a couple of PCs with giant dual-colored monitors. Fun times!

Now you can find many vocational schools, local workshops, or online services that can teach you to type quickly and efficiently using far better tools. You won't need correction tape when you make a mistake. And don't worry about the black ribbon running dry, because digital ink is limitless.

I'm grateful now for the time spent in typewriting class, because that skill has been the one I've used the most since my days in high school. Thankfully, I never gave up and pushed through the monotonous daily exercises that Mrs. Nagel gave us. Sure, learning to type was like watching paint dry, but it paid off in the long run.

CHOOSING THE RIGHT TYPING TOOLS & SOFTWARE

If typing is how you prefer to write, it's important to get good at it so you don't spend hours staring down your fingers and the sea of letters on the keys. However, there's still something to be said about that way of typing. A friend of mine types incredibly fast using just two fingers. He's great at it after years of practice.

I asked him one time if he'd ever considered learning the traditional way—left fingers on the A, S, D, and F keys and right fingers on the J, K, L, and semicolon keys. He didn't see any reason to change since he already typed at a pretty consistent pace.

Both ways have their pros and cons, but I recommend touch-typing if you want to type faster and more efficiently. With countless resources dedicated to touch-typing, you won't ever lack instructions or tools for improvement.

In fact, I use the site the Typing Speed Test to see how I've progressed. I hit about fifty-eight words per minute usually, give or take a few words. I could be a lot faster if I didn't constantly self-edit as I type. I practically wear out my backspace key and burn out my mouse going back to fix mistakes. The best way to improve is to keep going when you make a mistake and fix the issues in editing later on.

If you must change an entire sentence because it ruins the rest of your paragraph, then do it. Personally, I believe you should leave it and sort it out later. Push forward and write the best you can without hitting the backspace button constantly.

If you need word processing software, I recommend any of the following:

- Microsoft Word
- Apple Mac Pages
- Google Docs
- WPS Office
- Dibbly Create

What you write in doesn't matter as long as you have an auto-save feature and remember to create redundancies; this means saving your work in two locations like your computer's hard drive or a cloud-based service. If you already write using a cloud-based service, make sure you export your document every session and save it on your computer. If the cloud service fails, at least you have a backup.

As for hardware, use what you have available. A simple PC, Mac, tablet, or even mobile phone with a keyboard can do the trick. I prefer quiet-touch keys on a compact keyboard. However, if you have larger hands, that might not work for you. Shop around for options that best suit you.

Using a keyboard when typing on a mobile phone isn't essential, but I found that writing on my phone is leagues better when I do. You can find wireless keyboards that sync to smartphones or try the old-fashioned way by plugging into your phone's charging port. Depending on how old your phone is, this might be a challenge, but having an external keyboard will save your fingers over time.

Choose a keyboard that allows you to rest your palms on the tabletop comfortably while positioning your fingers in the optimal typing position. My fingers always hover over the keys in the middle row. Most keyboards will come with a little notch on the F and J keys, so you know where to place your index fingers without looking down. Get familiar with that notch so you don't have to look down repeatedly to know you're hitting the right keys.

IMPROVING TYPING SPEED & ACCURACY

If you're new to touch-typing or are just returning to it from a prolonged absence, give yourself some time to improve—not to mention a little patience and grace. Touch-typing is like exercising, reading, or any process requiring skill—you need to practice. If you don't practice, you'll never improve.

CHAPTER 2: SPEED TYPING TECHNIQUES FOR RAPID WRITING

Beyond the previously mentioned typing test, there are other ways to practice, such as writing every day consistently. You don't have to write your book; it can be something like an email, blog post, social media comment, you name it.

Setting a timer helps motivate me to type with no hesitation. Knowing that I have a deadline looming, I put the pedal to the metal and let my fingers do the talking. Then, when the time is up, I'll go back through and spot any typos I made. Errors will happen, and it's totally fine when they do.

Years ago, I took classical lessons on my nylon acoustic guitar. This was decades after learning to play guitar on my own, so I had to retrain myself to play correctly. The way I taught myself to play was inefficient and might have damaged my hands and wrists. One issue that would drive my instructor crazy was that I'd stop whenever I made a mistake, then start all over. He believed you should power through, stick with the tempo, then reflect on the mistake later.

He further assured me that if I continued to keep playing that way, I'd get stuck in a loop of refining the same part of a song over and over. Whereas if I looked at the complete structure of the song and stayed in time, I'd end up with a passable song. From there, I could identify where I went wrong and analyze my approach.

Teaching yourself to type better and more efficiently works the same way.

Try it out for yourself by writing a brief journal entry about how your day is going. Don't worry about writing to any audience beyond yourself. The point is to get into the habit of typing with no disruptions or interruptions. Aim to type without a break for about fifteen minutes.

I read about this theory in Kevin Tumlinson's *The 30-Day Author Plan*. This strategy involves setting a timer for fifteen minutes and reflecting on your day. Doing this exercise before writing a book helps grease your creative wheels and breaks the habit of endless editing. Remember, editing shouldn't come until after the first draft is complete. Anything else is premature, with few exceptions to the rule.

When I journal before my initial writing session, I am more efficient. I'm sure that comes down to not having any reader expectations in my head because I know I do not need to write perfect prose. In fact, I highly doubt I'll ever read my old journal entries. I have typed over 1,000 words in a session at times. Previously, I could type 300 words in fifteen minutes. After trying that journalling warm-up exercise, I can crank out 500 to 600 words every fifteen minutes.

IMPLEMENTING TIME-SAVING TYPING TECHNIQUES

The key to typing more efficiently is to practice daily for at least fifteen minutes or more. But I'd be remiss if I didn't tell you other ways to shorten your work time so you can type much faster.

When I first started typing, I didn't have the luxury of commands or hot keys. Now I have everything I could possibly need to ensure few interruptions. That's why you should have a basic grasp of common commands and quick keys that'll speed up your writing without sacrificing quality—or your sanity.

Almost every word processing program comes with a nearly universal set of commands that implement some type of shortcut when you strike a combination of two or more keys. For instance, if I need to move a misplaced sentence or section, I can highlight the passage with my mouse, then press the Ctrl key and the C key to copy that text or Ctrl plus the X key to cut it. Click your mouse on the place you want to move the clipped content, then press the Ctrl key and the V key to paste the text in the new location.

Another extremely helpful command is Find. If you press Ctrl plus the F key, a window will pop up on your document. Type a word into the small search bar to quickly find all uses of that word in your document. This helps whenever you might be stuck on a point or need to refer back to a previous chapter. Or, sometimes, you might feel you're repeating yourself, so a quick search will help clear your conscience of echoes so you can keep pushing forward.

Side note: For Mac users, replace the CTRL key with the CMND key.

Whenever I take a break from writing, even for just a few minutes, I always type "QQQ." If I close out the program and come back to it later, I know precisely where I stopped. Quite a few word processors will offer to pick up where you left off, but it's often hard to tell if you're in the middle of an idea. Those Q's bring my attention to precisely where I need to write, leaving no doubt about what I finished last.

This shortcut is also handy because it gives you a way to quickly search a document so you don't have to scroll endlessly through a long manuscript. Use the Find command (CTRL + F), then search for QQQ. Bingo! I'm right back where I stopped and can seamlessly jump back into my writing flow again.

Some software programs offer auto-correct and predictive text features. I'm not entirely a fan of auto-correct or predictive text, especially when I'm just trying to get the content out of my head and onto the digital paper. I feel like auto-correct and predictive text is like counting money while somebody yells out random numbers to throw me off. I'd rather not have the direction of my content dictated by automated systems. Instead, I prefer to grind it out and figure out the corrections and proper word choices later.

Another area of contention for newbie authors is how to format a manuscript properly. Do *not* sweat that until after editing, because you might needlessly format a manuscript that requires a complete overhaul, therefore squandering your time on an unnecessary task when what you need to do is produce a rough draft.

While I'm writing, I keep my formatting super simple:

- Body text is for the written content
- Headings are for the chapters and subchapters

If I break the content into subchapters, I'll typically scale down the headings. My main chapter uses the pre-set Heading 1 format in Word and my subchapter is Heading 2. Naturally, if the content breaks down any farther, I'd use Heading 3.

Also, most software you're using should have an auto-format feature that uses bullet points, numbers, or letters. If not, don't sweat it. You can sort that out later. As long as the points you're illustrating make sense, you should be good to push through and finish the draft.

Beyond that, formatting should be the last thing on your mind. Unless you're an avant-garde artist looking to blend prose with visual art, you don't have to sweat the interior design of your book.

For tables and graphs, type out the data or put a note to insert the data before sending the final draft to your editor. Don't bog yourself down with drafting intricate details right now. When you edit your book later, you can handle that. Otherwise, creating these types of elements is a time suck for your first draft.

While writing your book, just get the ideas out of your head and onto the paper. We'll manage editing and formatting later. Before we jump to those steps, let's analyze two other methods for writing your nonfiction book: voice dictation and transcribing.

CHAPTER 3:
VOICE DICTATION FOR EFFICIENT WRITING

Prior to my life as a full-time writer and video creator, I worked in assisted living communities. The older adults I worked with saw the value in learning how to use computers, but some had some mobility restrictions. This meant I had to find adaptive equipment to suit their needs.

One resident wanted desperately to email her grandkids, but arthritis pain and muscle atrophy hindered her hands. Teaching her to touch-type was off the table. Sadly, touch screens weren't in the budget, so I had to look into alternative means.

Enter voice dictation. Her son was gracious enough to buy the software Dragon Naturally Speaking 12.5 and a headset. All she needed to do was wear the headset, start the computer, and verbally express whatever she wanted to convey to her family. She had to train Dragon to understand her voice so it could accurately produce text of her words. Whenever the software produced the wrong word, she'd simply correct the program. It was then less likely to make that same mistake the next time she said the corrected word. The software came with a steep learning curve, but once we got past that, it was smooth sailing.

Dragon Naturally Speaking is still around today, but I hardly think it's worth the investment given all the free options out there. For instance, I wrote the entire introduction to this book with voice dictation using a browser extension called Speech Recognition Everywhere. It came with a 30-day trial, giving me ample time to find a suitable replacement elsewhere before the free trial period was up. It's not necessarily a tool I use today, but something worth considering if you're looking for free alternatives to Dragon.

If you're using your mobile phone to dictate content, a lot of programs like Google Docs and Microsoft Word are compatible with voice dictation. You can choose any method for dictating your book and aren't just limited to one.

The most important aspect of using voice dictation is to test it out and practice. Much like touch-typing, you're going to have to learn a new skill.

A few programs exist right now that intuitively know where to place punctuation, start a new paragraph, or add in dialogue. If you use tech that records your voice but does not input punctuation marks or paragraph separations, then that's not dictation—that's transcription.

When you use voice dictation programs, speak your words just as you would if you were typing. For instance, if you would type this:

I'm feeling great today! How are you?

You'd have to say this:

> *I'm feeling great today exclamation point*
> *how are you question mark.*

Years ago, I ghostwrote fiction short stories using voice dictation through Google Docs on my cellphone. All I had to do was press the mic icon on my virtual keyboard and speak out my words.

Voice dictating is a lot like writing with your non-dominant hand; it's a little awkward, and you'll feel slightly self-conscious as you go along. Don't let that derail you; it just takes practice.

In fact, *USA Today* bestselling author Nick Thacker shared how dictation may be an efficient means of writing, but that doesn't mean it's easy. In his course, *Dictation for Authors*, Nick breaks down some of the best ways to leverage voice dictation to produce content faster. In it, he explains that you'll produce quite a few errors, but the most important thing is to keep pushing forward. In the early edits, he relies on artificial intelligence to fix any misused words or grammar issues.

Again, being efficient comes down to honoring the order of things. Editing comes after the first draft and not any sooner, with few exceptions to the rule.

In terms of hardware, you'll need a decent microphone and a quiet space. Most onboard mics for mobile phones and laptops are more than sufficient. Even some cheap webcams come with a built-in mic. As you'd expect, you'll need to test the equipment to make sure it's accurately capturing what you say.

You shouldn't have to invest in an expensive microphone to get the job done. If you watch my YouTube channel, you'll often hear me using the Shure SM-7B. I don't recommend buying a $400 microphone if you're only planning to use it for voice dictation. That mic is great for podcasts and video production but overqualified for voice dictation. It's still usable, so who am I to complain?

You get bonus points if you record your voice dictation. This serves as a good insurance policy should things get a little hairy in the editing process. You can go back and review the recorded footage to clear up any misunderstandings.

Is it mandatory for you to record yourself while voice dictating? No, but having a redundancy in place could very well save your tail. For instance, if I voice dictate, I can live stream it to my YouTube channel. Once I'm done writing, I'll have that footage as a backup, just in case.

Will it be of use to anyone later? Possibly, but I don't make the backup for any other reason other than as a precaution. It serves the same function as creating redundancies of your manuscript on your computer and cloud drive.

REFINING YOUR VOICE DICTATION

Hopefully, you fully understand by now that typing and voice dictation take some work to perfect. You won't be able to dictate and type efficiently without practicing just like you couldn't simply use a keyboard for the first time and crank out thousands of words an hour. I'm sure world-famous basketball player Michael Jordan wasn't dunking his first day on the court, so you can't reasonably expect to dictate thousands of words per hour without a little experience doing it.

Programs like Dragon Naturally Speaking have their own set of rules and guidelines to "train" your dragon, so check their user manual for the best approach to their system. For the rest of you relying on an onboard or desktop mic, dictation will be a much simpler way of doing things that requires less work upfront but more work on the backend (i.e., in editing).

Here's a brief list of the commands you'll need to know so the words you speak don't come out as a giant wall of text:

Common words used for voice dictation include:

- "Period" for a period (.)
- "Comma" for a comma (,)
- "Question mark" for a question mark (?)
- "Exclamation mark" or "exclamation point" for an exclamation mark (!)
- "New line" or "Enter" for a line break
- "Tab" for an indentation
- "Open parenthesis" for a "("
- "Close parenthesis" for a ")"
- "Quotation mark" or "quote" for a quotation mark (")

This list isn't exhaustive; it's merely a starting point to illustrate what you need to say in order to dictate in complete sentences and paragraphs. These are just some of the frequently used words for voice dictation, and different software or applications may have variations or additional commands.

It will feel highly awkward at first to speak out a full sentence. If you practice long enough, you may find that you have a natural inclination for speaking out your sentences.

My biggest issue is that sometimes my brain gets caught up thinking about what I want to say next, and I forget to insert punctuation. Again, technology is certainly catching up so that authors can voice dictate without speaking the punctuation, but it's not entirely fleshed out just yet—unless you lean on transcriptions.

Should you plan to use voice dictation, you'll need to account for your own energy and stamina to complete the task. It's difficult to voice dictate for hours at a time. It can be tiring and often frustrating if you're new to the method.

Keep a glass of room temperature water nearby to keep hydrated while not restricting your vocal cords. I've even heard some folks will add a few squeezes of lemon to their tap water to aid performance. Personally, I just stick with regular water, nothing fancy.

Speak slowly and clearly while nearly exaggerating the pronunciation of a word. Think about it like speaking to someone with a hearing deficit. Shouting won't get you anywhere, but deliberate cadence and clear enunciation will help the program identify exactly what you're saying.

Enunciate with conviction. Speak as if you're talking through water, so there's no mistake about what you say. If you're prone to speaking fast, slow down until you've mastered the art of voice dictation. I'm a fast talker and often have to pump the brakes when I'm shooting videos.

Not everyone can tell what you're saying if you speak too fast. In the same way, voice dictation software needs a few milliseconds to decipher what you're saying.

If you want practice, I highly recommend spending two decades in the healthcare industry working with older adults with hearing issues. My experience in that field allowed me to work on my speaking voice and deliver what I said with confidence. Not everyone could hear me perfectly, but those who did knew precisely what I had said and the emotion I had projected. Even if the delivery feels a bit like acting in a Broadway play—project your voice and enunciate clearly.

OVERCOMING CHALLENGES & OPTIMIZING VOICE DICTATION

Now that you know voice dictation takes practice and time to master and that you have to articulate, let's make sure you put a few safeguards in place to make the most of your voice dictation session.

Get the mic as close to you as possible, around one to three feet away from your mouth. The perfect placement is directly in front of or just to the side of your face. If you have a lavalier microphone, then clip it to your collar and you're all set. Whether recording videos or voice dictating, I keep my mic roughly a foot in front of me and just below my chin. I place it there to avoid plosives—the *popping* sound made from certain letters or syllables.

Plosives can wreak havoc on your voice dictation since that powerful pop can distort what the software hears. Rather than hearing a word, it hears an explosion, then deciphers what it can. It's understandable that it might have a tough time comprehending what it hears if the sound is muddy.

The same goes with placing your mic too far away from your mouth. If you have a webcam for voice dictation but place it on the far side of an empty room, chances are likely that what the program provides won't match what you said.

You need to dictate in a noise-free environment. The space you choose doesn't have to be a professional studio or whisper room like you'd need for audiobook narration, but the space should be distant enough from other sounds so that your voice is the only recorded sound.

Some voice dictation programs pick up noise exceptionally well. In writing the first chapter of this book, I paused between paragraphs to formulate my thoughts. In that time, I muttered to myself, and the software picked up what I was saying. Though the dictation wasn't accurate, it was enough to potentially mess up my manuscript and create a whole lot of work in the editing later on.

Before dictating your book, have your outline ready and in front of you, so as you talk it out, you can knock down one item after the next with ease. Will you get it perfect every time? No. But again, with practice, you'll be flying along before you know it.

Should voice dictation be too much of a challenge and touch-typing is far outside your wheelhouse, then you need to consider the next best option—transcription. It's like voice dictation without all the commands.

CHAPTER 4:
TRANSCRIBING METHODS FOR FAST CONTENT GENERATION

Early in my writing career, I explored options to write more efficiently. Because of my extensive experience as an activities director in senior living communities, I've always had a pretty good handle on speaking. You get real good, real quick when you have older adults expecting you to speak clearly every time you talk.

Around 2015, I had the wild idea to outline my book like I normally would, but instead of typing, I'd speak it out. I was using a podcasting platform that would host audio files for me, so all I had to do was log in, hit the record button, and away I went. My little case study was going to cover my experience as a personal trainer called *The Consummate Fitness Professional*. Despite putting no effort into marketing and promotion, the ebook, paperback, and audiobook publications have earned thousands in revenue. Not bad considering how much I spent on it—more on that soon.

I had no previous plans to write a book about personal training, so I figured if the end product came out as complete garbage, I wouldn't be out more than some time and a little money.

Yes, I mentioned money. That might be a huge barrier for some authors who want to use transcription. Hang in there because there are some free alternatives, but they will require a little work.

While you speak your text and formatting into a voice dictation program, you're free from the shackles of transcription. All you have to do is record what you're saying, then hand off the audio file to a professional transcriptionist.

Let's start with the equipment and setting you'll need.

You'll need a microphone—again, nothing fancy. You absolutely must make sure what you record is clear and the words are discernible without having to crank up the volume. The mic placement here is much the same as voice dictation—one to three feet away from your mouth.

How you record will depend on what programs you're familiar with. You can use video capturing software or digital audio workstations. For my case study, I used an audio podcasting platform. It limited me to recording only one hour per day, so I ended up recording the whole thing in about three and a half sessions.

You can use live streaming platforms like YouTube to record yourself. If you're really self-conscious and don't want an audience, you can easily set the broadcast to private so no one ever sees it but you and the transcriptionist.

For those lacking a camera, consider the free open-source software Audacity for recording your audio tracks. Though it's a little overwhelming at first, you'll find quite a few tutorials on YouTube or other places online that explain how to use it. Just set the audio input to your preferred microphone and the audio output to your preferred listening device (i.e., headphones), click the record button, and go!

When you're finished, hit the stop button. After that, you can export the file to an .mp3 or .wav file and hand it off to a professional transcriptionist.

You will find from time to time that you'll misspeak or say something that comes out all wrong. Use my QQQ method for marking an area that needs addressing. Suppose you're speaking a paragraph and encounter a problem. Pause and say, "QQQ," so you can revisit and address it during the editing phase. Then, pick up where you left off and continue on.

The next step in the transcription process can work in one of two ways: transcribe it yourself or hire out. I don't recommend doing it yourself unless you absolutely have to based on budget restrictions. The process is as simple as recording the audio, then listening back and typing out what you hear. There'll be a whole lot of starting and stopping, especially if you're not a good typist.

Other free transcription solutions come through video and podcasting platforms like YouTube. Upload the audio file as an mp4—that means you'll need to produce it as a video—then wait for YouTube to auto-caption.

My good friend and serial entrepreneur Ben Gothard used to do it that way. He'd interview a guest, upload the video on YouTube, then download the auto-captioning file (also known as an SRT file). He then had to edit out the time stamps, form complete sentences with punctuation, and break up sentences and paragraphs so it wasn't a giant wall of text. The man became prolific pretty fast, but I can't even imagine the hours he put into transcribing all those interviews.

Should you have a deeper budget and less willingness to clean up a messy auto-captioned file, you can explore inexpensive services like Descript or Riverside. I gave Descript a trial run and found the output impressive. Other than a few mistaken words and some run-on sentences, it was fairly good for the price.

Riverside is another service you can use for getting decent transcriptions at about the same quality as Descript. I use Riverside for recording my podcast interviews since it captures the video and audio natively, so I get the best possible recording every time. It is accurate enough that you won't spend too much extra time cleaning up your transcription while editing.

Though the pricing will inevitably change after I publish this book, you can expect both services to range from $12 to $24 per month an annual plan or $19 to $35 on a monthly plan.

For anyone with a deeper budget and the need for more pinpoint accuracy, I highly recommend Rev.com. I used Rev for years to caption all my YouTube videos and only stopped using them more recently because of the volume of videos I produce across two channels. The cost can be exorbitant when you add it up.

Right now, Rev charges about $1.50 per minute for transcription. If you give them a sixty-minute audio file, that'll cost $90. Imagine if you're producing a 50,000-word manuscript that takes about five and a half hours to record. That's going to cost you $412.50.

That's a far cry from the free options and considerably more expensive than $12 per month for Descript or $9 per month for Riverside.

FM. What sets Rev apart from those services is its 99% accuracy guarantee. If they don't transcribe it accurately, they'll fix it for you at no cost. I had a couple of occasions when the transcript wasn't right, and Rev handled it right away. They have a cheaper option, but the output is about the same as what you get with the cheaper services.

You also pay for a quicker turnaround time. For instance, when I wrote this book, I started using voice dictation. Within the first two chapters, I realized I could not produce this manuscript in the allotted twenty-four hours. Instantly, I thought I could record the performance without the restrictions of voice dictation, send the file to Rev, and then just wait for them to send the file back.

One problem—a five- or six-hour audio file takes a few days to complete, possibly longer. I knew I wouldn't make it, having already spent ten percent of my time on voice dictation. Rev offers expedited service, but that would drive the cost up considerably.

I don't know about you, but I feel like at $400, the work better come back to me a lot faster. It's possible to get forty-eight-hour turnaround, but you'll have to pay out the nose. Let's be honest: You're done writing when you hit the stop button on your recording device, so technically, you can still finish your first draft in twenty-four hours.

The reality is once you get that file, you'll have to clean up your manuscript a bit, which moves you into the next step—editing. I guess that's a good thing, but how you view your book as a completed first draft is entirely up to your preference. I don't feel like I completed the manuscript if the transcript isn't in my hands within twenty-four hours.

CHAPTER 4: TRANSCRIBING METHODS FOR FAST CONTENT GENERATION

When I recorded the three and a half-hour transcript for my personal trainer book, I handed the audio files to an inexpensive transcriptionist on Fiverr. She must've desperately needed money, because it only cost me $35 per hour of content for a total cost of $112.50. She had the files back to me within a day or so, and they were highly accurate.

The nice part about working with a human transcriptionist is they'll remove any filler words (i.e., uh, um, etc.) you likely relied on while gathering your thoughts. If you stammer over a word, your transcriptionist will not type out repeated consonants or words. They'll instead trim it down to what reads the best.

Essentially, a human transcriptionist is your first editor. Browse the Fiverr marketplace for freelancers who provide transcription services. I stopped going there because Rev seemed far more qualified for what I wanted, and I didn't have to sift through an endless pile of options. I just provide Rev with the files and details they need to get started, and boom! All set!

Before you sink hundreds of dollars into a premium transcription service, read over their reviews and take them for a test drive. Start a gig with a page or chapter's worth of content. If that file comes back as you'd expect, then consider investing a larger sum. I never place too much trust in service recommendations, even if I am a hardcore fan of an influencer who swears by it. Expectations and experience vary wildly, so do your research before investing in anything.

That means the same thing for my recommendations. Yes, it'd be great for you to order from a service that I promote, but don't do it without fully investigating if it's the right option for you.

MAXIMIZING PRODUCTIVITY & ACCURACY WHEN TRANSCRIBING

It's possible that you have the inclination to record your entire book in one sitting. Unless you're producing an essay or pamphlet-length publication, spending more than an hour to two hours at a time can be exhausting. I recommend using the Pomodoro Method, where you speak for twenty-five minutes, then rest for five minutes and repeat for four rounds. After the last round, take a fifteen-minute break.

Speak clearly, but again, avoid shouting or projecting your voice too hard. You'll tire out and won't hit that one-day deadline. For me, transcribing and voice dictating are the best options for a twenty-four-hour writing challenge, but when you're not a proficient typist and need an avenue that works better, then work with what you have.

In a perfect world, you could record one to two hours of content per day until the book is complete. For a strict deadline, you're going to have to batten down the hatches, grit your teeth, and push through the fatigue (within reason).

While I tell you to speak clearly and enunciate, you also need to do it in a way that spares your voice for the long haul. It's probably a good idea to let your voice rest the day before and the day after recording, so you're not beating yourself up too much.

Another reason I recommend the Pomodoro Method is to force you to take a break to recover mentally and physically. You might find yourself wanting to rush through and rip the Band-Aid off, but I recommend taking the full break. Five minutes between each round and fifteen minutes between every four rounds really helps to recharge and reinvigorate your approach. So, take the breaks.

CHAPTER 4: TRANSCRIBING METHODS FOR FAST CONTENT GENERATION

Yes, you want to get the manuscript completed in as fast a time as possible, but you do not want to do it at the expense of your mental clarity and long-term focus on the project. Treat your breaks as seriously as you do the recording times. You'll thank me.

If I ever feel like my attention is waning, I simply change my position or move to another spot. This pattern disrupt is great to keep things fresh. I'm fortunate to have an electric adjustable standing desk, so when I need to stand up, I can do it with the press of a button. When I want to sit down, I can get there just as easily. If I were hard-pressed to change my scenery altogether, I could always use my tablet and find another quiet spot in my house or reserve a private study room at the local library—by the way, that's totally free at a lot of libraries.

Whenever I've written for at least four hours, I'll usually take a longer break. This is when I get some food, stretch a bit, and disconnect my brain from the book. It keeps my workflow fresh and makes the time go by so much faster.

If you're new to transcribing or voice dictating, try a two-hour test run. See how it goes and identify challenges you ran into. Also, gauge your energy levels, because when your energy is gone, the writing might suffer. A little trial and error in advance will go a long way if you want to write a nonfiction book in one day.

Set aside time to experiment with all three ways of writing: touch-typing, voice dictating, and transcribing. Once you find the method that works best for you, stick to it, practice, and give writing your next nonfiction book a shot in one day. If you fall short, you at least have a work-in-progress that you can build on after that initial day.

CHAPTER 5:
OVERCOMING TIME CONSTRAINTS AND INCREASING WRITING EFFICIENCY

While I've given you a few ways to write your nonfiction book in twenty-four hours, I haven't delved too deep into managing your time effectively and increasing productivity. Writing a book is a feat in itself. Now, add the complexity of doing it in one day and you've got quite a lofty goal. As expressed previously, don't try writing a book in a short time if it's at the detriment of your personal health and sanity.

A more efficient writer is a more prolific writer who will have a deeper backlog of books. Having a robust catalog of books under your author name provides additional avenues of exposure for you and your brand.

I often hear from authors who have produced only one book and saw no actual results. Yes, authors can succeed on many levels with one book, but those success stories are outliers in this business. Most folks are looking for something, anything, that resembles an answer to their problems. You might have one book that will scratch their itch, but having many books goes a long way toward instilling trust in you as an author.

If you want to be efficient and, by extension, more prolific, you have to really dial into what you're doing to complete your manuscript and push it through the additional steps to get it out into the market for sale.

In order to produce a manuscript in a day or less, you've got twenty-four hours to play with. However, you must be realistic about how well you'll perform that day, because nobody likes to burn the midnight oil when they're an early riser and vice versa. Sleep is absolutely a factor you must account for in those twenty-four hours.

I'm not the biggest proponent of caffeine or stimulants to get you up and keep you up for hours at a time. Though I used to consume mass quantities of caffeine, those days were over once I realized the inflammatory impact those stimulants had on my arthritis.

Even though I'll skip caffeine, I won't skip eating. I highly recommend you have food prepared the day ahead, so all you have to do is heat it up and eat. Heck, if you make foods that don't require heating, you've saved even more time.

Avoid junk food or processed foods since those will slow you down and gum up your system. This might be the former personal trainer coming out in me, but I highly recommend eating whole foods and anything that doesn't come in a package. Granted, everyone has certain tastes and diet restrictions, so research the best foods to provide you with needed sustenance and energy.

I'm a bit more experienced in the kitchen, so making a meal will take me about fifteen to thirty minutes. Most days, I eat at least three square meals between noon and ten at night. Outside of that window, I fast. That's my preference and is not my endorsement for everyone else to do intermittent fasting. I'm merely illustrating what my eating schedule is like from day to day.

Having food readily available should be your priority before jumping into a time-sensitive book project. Otherwise, you'll need to account for going to the store, being in traffic, standing in checkout lines, and any other elements out of your control.

To make the most out of your time, you absolutely must stay close to your writing workspace. Do not leave unless it's absolutely necessary. The more distractions I allow myself, the less likely I am to finish my work on time.

I am a full-time writer and video content creator, so this is my only job. I don't have to answer to a boss or worry about children. Beyond my two rescue cats and wife, I have nothing to derail my plans.

Authors with family to care for, daily responsibilities to attend to, and a day job that supplements your income until you can become a full-time writer will find that communication is paramount to the success of writing your nonfiction book in a day.

I understand that in certain situations, requesting free time might not be feasible because of your personal circumstances. In that case, writing for twenty-four hours of uninterrupted time might be a tall ask.

Ask anyway. Communicate the importance of having alone time so you can complete a project that's close to your heart and could very well help your family profoundly. If you have a partner and kids, ask your partner to tend to things for one day. After that day is up, you can pull your weight again.

Sure, you could prolong the writing process, but that would defeat the purpose of what you're learning in this book. You want to take massive freaking action and the only way to do that when you're balancing writer life and family life is with cooperation from everyone around you.

Also, there's an adage that'll serve you and others well in understanding—Parkinson's Law. The belief is that your work expands to fill the time allotted for completion. Let's say you set a deadline to complete your book within a year. You're more likely to focus on the minutiae or micro-elements of your book and fill your time with less important details that don't push your project forward.

Condensing the deadline creates a sense of urgency for the project. Rather than focusing on what covers you should make or how you're going to promote the book when you publish it, first devote all your time to finishing that first draft.

Consider this example. A person is given the task of sending a postcard. Normally, this action requires about three minutes. For some, that task might include time spent looking for their glasses, picking out the postcard, writing on the card, and putting it in the mailbox. Not to mention any other number of steps we'd normally take for granted.

Put that shorter window of time on a project and add some stakes, and it is much easier to cut out what doesn't serve your goal. Don't allow Parkinson's Law to wreak havoc over your plans. Plan the day ahead, and you'll set yourself up for victory. Part of that planning should include identifying potential distractions and potholes that could slow you down.

Nonfiction books typically run from 25,000 to 60,000 words. You can break that down to 1,041 to 2,500 words per hour. Keep in mind that you probably will not write the entire twenty-four hours, so you will need to increase your word count output considerably to finish in that timeframe.

Let's take away nine hours for sleeping, eating, and bathroom breaks. This leaves you about fifteen hours to write. This increases your hourly word count goal to 1,666 to 4,333. Now the pressure is on; you can see why eliminating needless distractions makes a tremendous difference.

Your daily online activities—like social media, emails, and web browsing—need to be curtailed for the entire day. Avoid jumping into time sucks during breaks. When I take a break between writing sprints, I avoid my computer altogether. I might turn on the TV briefly, but I purposely choose programs or videos that won't hook me and keep me past my allotted break time.

This can be brutal if you're used to keeping your presence online active. For one day, you have to shut it off. They'll be there when you come back. You may also want to consider taking off the next day, because trust me, writing a book in one day is challenging and may exhaust you. Hopping right back into the fray of social media or the onslaught of emails isn't the healthiest way to reward yourself for a job well done.

Consider other ways of rewarding yourself, like going out for a walk or bike ride, or even visiting with some friends. Do anything that doesn't involve a computer or mobile device.

Your chief priority in that day's time is writing the book—that's it. Anything other than eating, sleeping, resting and, of course, writing, should *not* be your priority. If you want to get it done in a day, writing needs to be the top priority.

ELIMINATING DISTRACTIONS & MAINTAINING FOCUS

You've learned about the various distractions and potential interruptions in your day, but now it's time to put pen to paper. Before you even consider writing your book, you'll need to pick a day and time to start your project. Identify potential issues you might run into, whether in your day job or because of family responsibilities.

When planning out the day to write this book, I scoured my already busy schedule for the most opportune slot. It just so happens that I keep my Fridays clear so I can finish my tasks for the week and focus on last-minute admin work before the weekend starts. I work a light day on Saturdays and take Sundays off. When I return to work on Mondays, I'm typically slammed, so putting all my weekly chores on hold isn't very realistic.

As a video content creator, Tuesday through Thursday are heavy with news items and relevant information, so I don't schedule any major projects on those days because my needs can change in an instant. Choosing Friday for writing set me up for success since that is the day I naturally have the most flexibility in my schedule.

The next thing I had to do to get ready to write this book in one day was finish all my grocery shopping, so I had plenty of time to prep meals and have food ready for my breaks. Any other daily chores I normally would do on Fridays got bumped to the day before or after. That created a little extra stress and anxiety, but since I was knocking down a monumental task in one day, I was also sparing myself weeks, if not months, I might otherwise have toiled over a first draft.

When you list specific issues that are outside of your control, figure out the best way to cope with them, but don't get too stuck in hypotheticals. Remember, you're just looking for potential situations and mitigating those the best way you can. In dire emergencies—like my cat needing to be rushed to the vet clinic—I know I will have to pull the plug. The chances of that happening are pretty slim since my cats are just over two years old. Years from now, that might be a different story. For now, it's not even remotely going to be an issue.

Since you'll be writing for hours at a time, it's vital you put yourself in a setting that nurtures your writing spirit. I have a home office where I have an adjustable standing desk, three monitors, two large bookshelves, and a gamer's chair. Add a bit of lighting to set the mood, and I'm ready.

You're going to need to design a space, even if it's temporary, where you will be excited at the prospect of writing. When you can feel genuinely thrilled to write, it makes the hardcore commitment of writing for one day straight so much easier.

I can't imagine being very productive if my writing space was a packed coffee shop with a whole lot of distracting comings and goings. That's a personal taste, so if that environment suits you, run with it. My wife, Kelli, loves to visit different coffee shops because the change of scenery inspires unrivaled focus that she doesn't get from working at home. There's no one right place to write, as long as it serves your end goal of writing productively and efficiently.

CHAPTER 5: OVERCOMING TIME CONSTRAINTS AND INCREASING WRITING EFFICIENCY

I completed this manuscript as part of a *24-Hour Book Writing Challenge* video for my YouTube channel. I had someone hold me accountable by checking in at 11:00 a.m. on Friday and Saturday. After I checked in, you'd think I jumped straight into writing. That's far from the truth.

I started my day with a workout and breakfast. Right after that, I checked in, but I was feeling a little stressed and anxious. Rather than jumping into writing and forcing a square peg into a round hole, I decided the best way forward was to take one step back. I took a half hour to meditate so I could clear my mind and free up some of that anxious energy.

I'm not insinuating that you need to join a religion or follow some yogi's practice high atop the mountains in Nepal. Meditation is essentially a way of disconnecting from the outside world; it's like fitness for the mind. I do not go a day without meditating for at least fifteen minutes, because it clears my head and gives me razor-sharp focus.

Sure enough, as soon as I was done, I felt a little better and popped into writing this book. Could I have skipped it? Yes, but I feel my work would've suffered. Knowing how I function under stress has served me well. I had to take one step back to take two steps forward.

After that, the words came pouring out of me like a geyser.

To meditate and get into the right mindset to write a book in twenty-four hours, all you need is a quiet space and somewhere to relax. Most people will sit cross-legged in the lotus pose, while some folks prefer lying flat and elevating the head and knees. I'll typically play an ambient soundtrack that lasts the duration of my session, so when I hear it finish, I know my time is up.

The hard part is disconnecting. I prefer to focus on nothing but my body—any aspect will do, like my breathing or a specific body part. When a thought comes floating in, I send it on its way and go back to my focus exercise. During some sessions, I'll get derailed dozens of times. In others, I become so relaxed, I fall asleep.

If you are new to meditation, practice it before using it as a tool to steady your mind. New practitioners will fall asleep, so setting a gentle alarm to wake you might be a safeguard to consider. You don't want to start your one-day writing session by sleeping through half of it.

Just like working out, meditation is a mental exercise that you can never perfect. As long as you're consistent and reflect on your progress, you'll reap the rewards through greater mental clarity and concentration.

SETTING REALISTIC GOALS & DEADLINES

I think we can all agree that writing a book in a day is a rather lofty goal, and, for some folks, this will feel nearly impossible. That's why you'll need to be self-aware enough to know whether writing a book in twenty-four hours is realistic for you or not. Before you toss out the idea, at least give it a shot. You never know what you're capable of when you put your mind to it.

I'm a big proponent of goal setting. No, you don't need some fancy workbook or an overpriced course to tell you how to set goals. It's simple when you consider what we're talking about here—writing a nonfiction book in twenty-four hours.

You know you have a sound goal when it fits perfectly into the S.M.A.R.T. goals philosophy. This acronym represents goals that are:

1. Specific: You can get a bit more specific beyond just a nonfiction book. That's why I started this book by discussing what to write. Get specific about the type of nonfiction book you're writing and who it's for.
2. Measurable: How long the book you want to write is up to you. I gave you some general guidelines for a full-length nonfiction book, but no one is forcing you to adhere to a specific word count, especially if you're an indie author.
3. Attainable: Is this something that you or anyone else you know has done before? Chances are likely, yes. Again, analyze potential obstacles that could prevent you from reaching your goal and develop solutions so you can finish the project.
4. Relevant: If you're a writer and you're focusing on writing more books, mastering fast and efficient writing—like completing a book in twenty-four hours—is absolutely relevant to you.
5. Time-bound: Hey, your work is already cut out for you on this point. If you planned out your meals, breaks, and brief commercial interruptions, then you should still be able to get the job done in the twenty-four hours you're budgeting to finish a first draft.

I don't expect you to write each part of that goal down, but if it helps cement it into your subconscious, then do it. I prefer to jot down my goals on a daily checklist. I understand to-do lists don't work for some people, but it's been highly effective in corralling my ADHD behaviors.

If at any point you feel overwhelmed, take a breather, meditate, and look at the bigger picture. I often ask gridlocked authors this question:

How do you eat an elephant? One bite at a time.

Focus on completing one piece of your work at a time and avoid hyper-fixating on the summit of your project. Yes, that's going to take a lot of effort. The best way to burn through is one word at a time. Take a deep breath and just push forward when the overwhelm creeps in.

Nobody expects you to be perfect in your first draft. Just get it done, then you can worry about adding, subtracting, or deeply editing the manuscript later.

CHAPTER 6:
MOTIVATION AND CONFIDENCE IN COMPLETING A NONFICTION BOOK

Now that you've got your outline prepared, your time set aside, and your family informed, there's one potential pitfall that could ruin everything: you. Yes, you can be your own worst enemy, clogging up the process and slowing everything down to a crawl.

Writing an outline is simple as long as you're thoroughly versed in the subject you're writing about. Setting aside time becomes a little more complex, especially when considering all your activities of daily life. While it might be tough to enlist your family's support for this major undertaking, finding a balance that accommodates everyone's needs and respects your writing time should make it possible.

But when the time finally comes, the flashing cursor on-screen might make you lose everything you wanted to say and how you'd like to say it. Whether you want to call this self-doubt or writer's block, anything preventing you from doing your job can derail everything.

One of my favorite nonfiction authors, Honoree Corder, recently published a book called *There's No Such Thing as Writer's Block*.

Don't let the title fool you; she gives practical advice and tips for overcoming writer's block.

Honoree shares the same view as many other authors who have the luxury of pouring out word after word of endless prose. Meanwhile, some of us feel hamstrung, trapped in our own way. Offering condescending advice like, "Is there such a thing as plumber's block?" or "Is there such a thing as (insert profession)'s block?" may seem like a good point. The problem with that perspective is that writing and plumbing are very different professions requiring a distinct set of skills. Writing requires much more creative energy and one of the most vital ingredients of any prolific author—confidence.

I won't tell you writer's block isn't real. If you're stuck and you don't know why, take a step back and analyze. What is preventing you from putting words on the page? Are you stymied by your inner editor's constant interjections? Have you worked up such a grandiose vision of your finished project that getting it down seems like an impossible task?

Whatever is stopping you from putting pen to paper needs addressing from a rational mind, almost like a third-party perspective. Be bold enough to give yourself the same advice you'd give anyone else in your position. Hopefully, it's not a message of defeat or a recommendation to quit.

The time you need the most support is when you're writing your first draft. Doubt is a dangerous weapon that can easily neutralize all your future writing plans. When you're not producing words, stop and ask yourself why.

CHAPTER 6: MOTIVATION AND CONFIDENCE IN COMPLETING A NONFICTION BOOK

What is truly stopping you from writing your book? My former therapist once shared this with me about how the brain functions: Previous traumas have a way of creating issues in your life in ways you might not suspect. It's like driving a car with a crying child in the backseat. Merely yelling at the kid to shut up will only make it worse. Ignoring the child won't make it go away.

Do the right thing: Pull the car over to attend to that child.

I'm in no position to tell you how to address trauma. That's what a qualified therapist is for. If confidence is damaging your ability to write, identifying the problem will go a long way toward preventing obstacles to your writing over the long term. Once you identify the issue, figure out how to best resolve it.

Most times, it's just as simple as taking a leap of faith—start writing. I previously shared one method I use is journaling for fifteen minutes prior to writing. Another similar way is to write about anything, no matter how jumbled it is. Treat your writing like a conversation with your reader. In real life, you won't normally get stuck on what to say if the person listening knows you have details they want to hear more about.

Sure, how you communicate might not be the best, but at least you're putting in the effort to carry a conversation. Can you imagine asking someone a question and that person just stares at you, struggling for an answer? It's quite awkward but doesn't happen too often. Most of the time, people will at least entertain each other with small talk until the conversation pivots to more exciting topics.

Start out your writing with small talk. Maybe share a story that relates to your niche in some capacity. Think about a time when you learned an invaluable lesson that illustrates the value of your insights. You don't have to overthink this part.

Give your inner editor the night off because he's not just unwelcome but barred from attending this twenty-four-hour writing project. In a lot of instances, that's what prevents writers from writing—the inner editor or the compulsive need to make things perfect on the first try.

It's funny that the sentence you've written and rewritten a thousand times was probably its best the first time. Newbie authors often try to write overly complex sentences, not making them better but worse overall.

Sometimes, the easiest way to write it is to say it. Type out what you're thinking, and before you even edit it, read it aloud. Then, analyze it objectively. If someone said this sentence to you, would it work? Do you clearly understand what is being said? If so, it's fine, let it ride. Again, when you're stuck trying to perfect a sentence, you're losing valuable time you could put toward finishing the project. Sort out your hang-ups in the editing phases.

Indie author Martin McConnell has a short yet impactful book on breaking writer's block called *Finish the Damn Book!* Unlike Honoree, he validates the existence of writer's block, gives unending motivation and inspiration, and sends you on your way to write your next book. The best part about his book is you don't have to read it from front to back. He built each chapter with several solutions to get the words flowing consistently and smoothly. I highly recommend picking up a copy.

CHAPTER 6: MOTIVATION AND CONFIDENCE IN COMPLETING A NONFICTION BOOK

USING POSITIVE REINFORCEMENT & VISUALIZATION

Under normal circumstances, I usually eat three meals a day, with a couple of occasional snacks. Rarely do I deviate from my daily routine. My one exception is when I need extra focus for my writing. When the finished manuscript is simply not enough to light my wick, I have to add some positive reinforcement.

I love nuts and smoothies. Realizing both these foods are calorie dense, I try to eat them sparingly. When I do, I use them as a small reward—a bit of positive reinforcement. When I started my day writing this book, I went to the store and grabbed a smoothie and three small bags of nuts.

When I finish at least three chapters, I give myself a nice little treat. It works even better when I only eat during my brief breaks under the Pomodoro Method. Rather than grazing on my snacks while I write, I save them for when I'm free. Rewards work well, as long as you're not wasting writing time.

Even though I finished my second set of three chapters during my writing sprint, I waited to enjoy my reward until the time was up and I was on a break. By the way, having little rewards waiting for you at every break is a genius way to force yourself to take those breaks.

Now, I'm not insinuating you have to reward yourself with edibles and treats. Figure out what is a great reward for you. Maybe you get your partner to pay you ten bucks every time you finish two hours of writing. Or you get one grand prize for completing everything, like a day at the spa or a night out at a comedy club. How you reward yourself is completely up to you.

Some folks have the discipline to view the end goal as the reward, but others like me enjoy the self-praise and positive reinforcement that near-instant gratification provides.

I'm sure many great authors have their own rewards systems, so search around and find out what drives them to write consistently with unbridled enthusiasm. Incredibly successful authors from Stephen King to E.L. James have generously shared their writing processes. Study them. They know what they're doing, and that's clear from the empires they've built.

No one way is going to fit everyone, so it might take some self-exploration to figure out what compels you to push forward when times get a little tough. When you're working in a brief window of time, you will face some moments where you question why you even did this.

Side note: I'm feeling it now. The good news is I have a reward and a bit of positive reinforcement waiting for me in another three chapters. That excitement, however small, will fuel me enough to reach the next milestone.

Figure out what'll move you from one milepost to the next when you're feeling at your lowest—whether creatively or mentally.

BUILDING A SUPPORT SYSTEM & SEEKING ACCOUNTABILITY

I'm fortunate to be in the position I am with over 100,000 followers across multiple social media platforms. Whenever I need a pick-me-up or a little accountability, I just say so to my audience.

The last thing I expect you to do is build a following just so you have a support system and a little accountability for your writing projects. If you already did your homework by sharing with your family your desire to write a book in a day, then chances are likely they are your built-in support system.

However, you can supercharge that support system by networking with other authors. You get bonus points if that author writes in the same niche as you. Finding other authors seems difficult in theory, but it's actually quite simple in practice. Though what I'll share might seem abstract, it really isn't, considering how easy it is to connect with people these days.

Look for where your people congregate. Your people are the ones who love your type of content or revere your craft. If you're a sports fanatic, then go where other sports fans hang out. The next step is the hardest: Introduce yourself and get to know other people.

Let's not overcomplicate this task with too many moving parts. It's really as simple as stepping out from behind your desk and truly connecting with your ideal audience.

Next, you can tap into a vast array of author-based forums and groups. For instance, I have a community for authors on Discord where we cover everything from keywords to Amazon Ads to marketing and beyond. Quite a few authors have built long-lasting relationships which lead to more support.

Ideally, you need to find an author who can hold you accountable. It works well if that person needs the same in return. The reciprocal exchange goes a long way.

For instance, when you share your goals and specific deadlines with them, your accountability partner can follow up with you at random intervals. Once they deliver on their end of things, you're more inclined to reciprocate the favor. Keep the goodwill train rolling when your partner needs it most through a kind word or a gentle follow-up on the progress of their book.

When writing my book *Networking for Authors*, I had my writing mentor Jeanne De Vita in the loop on what I was doing and the deadline I set. She was so sweet in shooting me a few texts, checking in on my progress. She didn't have to do it, but, boy, did it help keep me on track.

Other ways you can find accountability partners are through local writers' workshops or conferences. I've attended quite a few in-person conferences, and each time I leave with some new friends. Anyone working on a tight budget might not have the luxury of attending premium in-person events, so that's when you have to do a little more digging. My wife has an uncanny ability to discover the best free events an author could want in our local area. It usually requires a simple search of the type of event in our geographical area. We've found quite a few opportunities through the website MeetUp.com. Don't sleep on that platform to find the best local events.

If you're an author who'd rather eat broken glass than meet people at in-person events, then virtual events are your next best options. How do you find them? Just ask around. Virtual summits are practically a dime a dozen. I'd say everyone and their mother runs a virtual conference these days and that might be accurate—except I don't think my mom would bother with it.

Some of these virtual events have mixers through group video chats hosted on Zoom or any virtual conference hosting platform like Hopin. In the video creator space, I joined a virtual mixer that was a blast. The host divided the guests into five different virtual rooms, giving everyone ten minutes to chat in the room before mixing up the rooms and starting over. Because things moved quickly, people felt compelled to share the best parts of themselves.

There truly is no single way to connect with other people. Though it seems like an arduous and unfulfilling task to some, I, and many other successful authors, have found networking is the secret ingredient that unlocks amazing opportunities. The benefits extend far beyond support and accountability. All you have to do is get out there and meet some people.

CHAPTER 7:
POLISHING YOUR MANUSCRIPT FOR PUBLISHING

You've learned everything you need to know to produce a nonfiction manuscript in twenty-four hours, so what comes next? Originally, I didn't think sharing the next steps would be essential, but I feel like this book would be incomplete without them. Everything from this point on is what comes after the twenty-four-hour writing marathon. Let's get your manuscript showroom ready and out into the world so you can reap the rewards from your focused and deliberate efforts.

I've teased this topic throughout the entire book: editing. I'll spare you the micro details and will focus on a more macro view of the next phase. You'll get enough information to take the steps necessary to clean up your book for an eager audience.

To be clear, you should never publish a book without putting it through many layers of editing and proofreading. Since you're so close to the book, bias clouds your vision of typos, grammatical mistakes, and everything else that can make your book less than great.

First off, put some distance between you and your manuscript after completion, especially if you just ran a marathon to get it done. The quickest path to burnout is to run back-to-back marathons over and again. You will need to pass your book through numerous rounds of edits before it's done. Even the best authors in the world rely on a deep editing process.

Once you've allowed at least a day to pass since finishing your manuscript, it's time to get to work on what I lovingly call the self-edit. You should edit your own book, but this also implies you're going to need to lean on an outside party to edit after you.

I have three steps for cleaning up my book:

1. Microsoft Editor. I use this tool to identify any typos, grammar issues, and syntax errors quickly. Though this grammar checker isn't 100% accurate or foolproof, it gives you the option to pinpoint minor problems.
2. ProWritingAid. Then I feed my manuscript through a grammar-checking tool that includes an array of reports to analyze your writing for areas of improvement. For instance, I'm guilty of writing passive sentence structure, echoes, and wordy sentences. This tool offers reports that address each of those problems. On my first pass, I use the Real-Time report to uncover anything the previous Editor didn't.
3. Text-to-Speech (TTS). Tools like Microsoft Word can read written content to you in the style and speed you prefer. Premium services like Speechify integrate with a variety of software and online tools, so there's another option. When you listen to your content, avoid reading along. Just listen.

When you hear something that sounds off, pause the voice, then make the correction in the text. Remember to play the corrected passage to see how it sounds.

On my first self-edit, I'm not focused on adding or subtracting content. I already outlined and wrote the content. Rather than allowing the perfectionist in me to feel it needs more work, I'd rather have third-party confirmation. No sense in creating a bunch of extra work that may get thrown out.

Sending a raw first draft to an editor is going to eat up their precious time, therefore costing you more. Rather than focusing on surface-level mistakes, I want my editor worrying about the structure, the flow, and how the book reads as a whole. I don't want to waste another person's time with all the blemishes in my manuscript.

Once I've done these three fast-pass self-edits, I go to a human editor. Yes, I didn't say a grammar checking software or some AI-derived editing tool. A human editor has insights and experience that'll bring out the best in your manuscript.

Once you find a good editor, you'll become more efficient the more projects you work on together. The editor for my first five books on self-publishing was Ava Fails. With every finished project, I always knew what she expected in a clean manuscript, but she always raised those standards with each new book. Her keen eye for detail was second to none, and the proof is in the finished product. Those five books went on to collect over two dozen book awards.

I highly doubt I would've accomplished even a fraction of that if left to my own devices.

In the first round of edits, you'll want a developmental or structural editor. They're going to look at the big picture of your book, making sure everything is in the right order and the flow is smooth. They will identify any holes in your book worth filling.

You'll get your manuscript back with notes and will need to make changes. Do you have to adhere to all your editor's notes? No, but any note made is worth considering. Editors only care that your book is at its best. They're not meaning to tear you down but build your book up so it can be the absolute best version it can be. You'll have to learn how to take constructive criticism. If you don't take it from your editor, you'll be forced to take it from dissatisfied readers.

If your book sells but readers stop buying your next books with complaints about editing, that editor is out of a job. Sure, take all advice with a grain of salt, but in the same instance, you are leaning on them for their expert insights and experience.

After I clean up any structural issues, I'll do another round of the three original passes of self-edits. Yes, I still find mistakes and issues. Don't skip these steps; they're totally worth the extra hassle.

Then I'll send my manuscript for copyedits. The copyeditor will tear apart sentence structure, grammar use, and other areas that weaken my writing. ProWritingAid helps me handle most copyediting issues, but it's not 100% accurate at catching everything. That's why another set of human eyes will go a long way.

Once you get the manuscript back, make all the edits, and as you'd guess, repeat the three quick passes. This manuscript is nearing completion, but we've got two, potentially three, more rounds to hit.

My next step is to go to a beta reading team. These readers specifically read your manuscript to offer raw feedback and insights you might not have considered. Some authors will use beta reading instead of developmental editing since the readers on your team should be well-versed in your niche.

You'll want at least one reliable beta reader to work with, someone who'll be happy to read your book and give you candid feedback. You don't want a reader who comes back and simply says, "That's perfect!"

You need someone bold enough to be honest yet tactful. For my fiction writing, I have three authors who write in my niche, so they're deep into the same type of writing. When they point out flaws, I know it's coming from a good place and is feedback worth considering. For my nonfiction writing, I've tapped into my community and sorted out three solid readers I can lean on.

When selecting a beta reader, you must set expectations out of the gate. Don't go into it assuming your beta reader knows what you want. You need to be blunt about what you expect and if they can't meet those needs, you'll have to find somebody else.

Michael La Ronn, host of the YouTube Channel formerly known as *Author Level Up*, hires beta readers from freelance websites. He searches for readers intimately familiar with his niche and pays them, so he knows he's going to get his feedback in a timely fashion.

It's been my experience that when relying on a volunteer army, there will be turnover. I'm sure there are many exceptions to the rule, but I want to temper your expectations with reality. Some folks' lives change for the better or worse and your books won't be their priority anymore. That's okay.

Either way, you choose—whether hiring beta readers or scouting out volunteers—you can't go wrong with this step. A great beta reader will always pick out items you and your editors missed.

Once you receive the notes, revise, repeat the three passes, and then proceed to the last step—proofreading. Consider proofreading as your last defense. It's going to polish your work and get it showroom ready. Some authors will insert proofreading after formatting the manuscript. However, that can get costly quick if you're hiring out interior formatters (more about that later).

I've found good proofreading through freelance services like Fiverr or even through the indie author community. When I prepared to launch my fitness book, *The Stretch Workout Plan*, I leaned on three authors to read it. They weren't fitness authors, merely other sets of capable eyes that could pick out any issues or mistakes. They pointed out things like typos or incorrect word choices.

Once you get the notes back from your proofreaders, make all the corrections. Then it's finally time to format your manuscript.

There is one last step, but this is certainly not mandatory for everyone: an advance reader copy (ARC) team. These readers get access to your book before it launches in exchange for posting an honest review online. Review gathering should be a large part of every author's marketing plan. Social proof goes a long way toward convincing potential readers to become buying customers.

Load your ARC team up with as many people as you can. Avoid friends and family because they're probably not your ideal reader. You want to recruit only hungry and voracious readers who'll tell the world about you, both good and bad.

On average, about 30% of ARC team members will post a review upon publishing.[ii] It's the sad reality that only about three out of ten people you recruit will follow through. Don't take this the wrong way. Often something came up in their lives that was a bit more important than posting a review for your book. It's not your business what they do outside of your book, so don't stress when a team member doesn't fulfill their volunteer commitments. Make a note to avoid bringing that person on for your next project and move on.

The more readers you have on your beta reading and ARC teams, the more likely someone will identify any lingering mistakes. Inevitably, after all those rounds of edits, something will slip through. Even though your manuscript has gone through many hands, it's still common to miss an issue or two. Just politely request that your team send you any errors or problems they find.

If you build your ARC team well enough in advance, some readers will provide you with an early access review. There, you'll get an even more candid look at how they feel about your book.

While you might think you're done with the edits, there is one absolute last layer of protection: your audiobook narrator. They'll pick out any weird wording issues and typos. When you hire a narrator, request that they send you the notes of what they had to update to make the manuscript more readable. If you're the narrator, you'll definitely find some issues.

Months after I launched *The Amazon Self-Publisher Series*, I recorded the audiobooks. I had to stop and make notes a few times. Again, you'll find mistakes after your manuscript has passed through many hands. If you're an indie author, this is an easy problem to fix. Publish the content and expect to upload a corrected manuscript a couple times after launch.

COSTS & EXPECTATIONS OF EDITING

Can you get away with publishing books by self-editing alone? Sure, but considering all the evidence I shared about how a manuscript can still have issues after three dozen people have reviewed it, you see how outside editors are a vital part of the process of publishing your book. Skip this step, and you'll face the consequences when you get low reviews that cite editing as a major issue.

The current rates for editing as of 2024 are roughly:

- Developmental Editing = $0.028 per word or $45-$66 per hour
- Copyediting = $0.021 per word or $35-$55 per hour
- Proofreading = $0.015 per word or $30-$45 per hour[iii]

As with any service, check the editor's portfolio, client testimonials, and any reviews. You'll want an editor with extensive experience in your field, so they can fact-check your work. Is it paramount to get an editor familiar with your niche? No, but it certainly goes a long way toward creating the best book for your ideal reader.

Once you feel you've found a good professional to do your editing, have them provide a sample edit of a brief passage, like a few pages or a full chapter. Once it's a lock, provide the rest of the project. You won't have to vet editors often because once you find a good one, chances are likely you'll work with each other for years to come. I don't bother with the test run on subsequent books since I already know how the editor works.

As mentioned previously, beta readers and proofreaders don't have to cost money, but at least you have a ballpark range on how much it might cost to hire out.

The worst-case scenario is that you can't afford to hire a professional. What do you do then? Remember how I mentioned all authors should build a network of other business professionals? There's your ticket. For every one cash-strapped author, there's at least a dozen others with the same problem. Why not work together?

Is that the ideal solution? No. Should you wait to raise the funds to afford an editor? That's your call. As long as you don't rely on yourself to edit alone, you should be fine. I recommend if you skip hiring a pro once, use the revenue from book sales to fund the next project.

In a perfect world, authors could write a killer first draft and publish it, but we live in anything but a total Utopia. That's why it's critical to lean on outside parties to help bring out the best in you, so readers will get exactly what they've always wanted—a well-written nonfiction book with the exact answers they've always needed.

CHAPTER 8:
PUBLISHING OPTIONS

N ow it's time to publish your work, but where do you begin? Many authors aspire to land the much-coveted spot of a traditional publishing (trad pub) deal with one of the Big Five publishers. While that's a wonderful dream to have, the reality is you're competing with hundreds of thousands of authors to get the attention of a major company. These days it takes so much more than a well-written book to land a trad pub deal.

Agents and acquiring editors look for an author who has an established following and has proof of concept. Trad pub companies are looking for talented and tenacious writers who are out there hustling their faces off, building an army of raving fans.

Why? Because they feel they'll get a return on their investment should they sign you as an author.

Getting a trad pub deal takes a lot of time, patience, and persistence. These days, in order to submit your manuscript to a traditional publisher, you need an agent to represent you. Finding an agent can be equally tough because you usually need a very large social media following or proof of concept. Literary agents take a percentage of your earnings, and given that the average literary agent receives 3,000-5,000 submissions every single month, the odds of your work being picked up are miniscule.

Yes, trad pub will pay you, but advances and royalty rates are absurdly low compared to self-publishing, which allows you to collect the lion's share of profits. Agents are not just being greedy; they have to account for staffing, overhead, and the time to develop your book into a project they can market.

Traditional publishers handle all the editing, formatting, book cover design, and marketing—including writing a book description—so all you have to do is provide them with what they ask for. After they publish your book, they may have a marketing budget to push your title for a limited time. In the fast-moving world of book publishing, what's hot now won't be hot later, so they'll move onto other things—unless your name is Dean Koontz or JK Rowling. Those outliers are the wildly successful authors that trad pub companies know they can invest in because they'll continue to get a return on their investment.

The rest of marketing and promotion is up to you. Get out, make media appearances, do the interviews, and appear at local bookshops for readings or signings.

Remember how the trad publisher handled a lot for you? When you self-publish, you handle all that and more! Trad pub companies have the benefit of deeper budgets, experienced professionals, and a team that works like an assembly line for books. Their job is to polish and perfect their publications, then launch them. Yes, it takes longer to put a book through the trad pub system, but that's because there are more hands in the production, and that slows everything down.

Self-publishers wear all the hats. If there is something you can't do, you'll have to hire a professional to handle it. While you're making a higher profit per book sale, you'll need to use those earnings to fund future publications and to sustain your author platform.

You also determine the speed at which you write, edit, format, and then publish a book. No need to wait half a year to two years or more like traditionally published authors often do. You can write a book in twenty-four hours, then follow all the steps I have shared and have that title out on the market within months, if not weeks. People often assume speed means producing low-quality work because of the belief that slow traditional publishers set the standard for book publishing.

That doesn't have to be true. Traditional publishing companies have thousands of assets to manage simultaneously, whereas an indie author only has to worry about what's in front of them.

I'm one of the growing numbers of authors who prefer staying independent. I left my day job so I didn't have to answer to anyone, so pursuing a trad pub deal doesn't quite align with my goals. That doesn't mean you should wholeheartedly agree with me. If it's your dream to get signed by a trad pub company, then go for it. Just know that you have many hurdles to clear before you can even expect to be seen by the right people in the right positions.

I'd rather not put on the dog and pony show, instead opting to publish what I want, when I want, and get paid my actual value for it. For the sake of comparison, many traditional publishing contracts offer an average royalty rate of 10%. That means you're only getting $0.10 out of every net dollar earned.[iv] For self-publishing, the average royalty is as high as 75%. These are rough numbers, and the royalties fluctuate based on the publication type: digital, print, or audio.

Distribution is a bit more favorable for trad pub companies since most retailers view those books as superior. It's not a fair assessment, but you'll see favoritism at play in places like Amazon and the local Barnes & Noble Bookstores. I'm sure these companies work out special deals in order to stock their books on shelves, so it's not surprising that when you go with trad pub, you'll have better positioning.

However, don't take self-publishing for granted because there are more distribution options than ever: Amazon KDP, IngramSpark, Draft2Digital, and dozens more. Can you get your book into brick-and-mortar stores? Sure, but you'll need to make it happen through person-to-person contact and networking.

Ingram Book Group fulfills print orders for quite a few distribution companies, and part of their reach includes brick-and-mortar stores. Just because they make your title available to stores doesn't guarantee you'll get placement. Store owners need a solid reason to buy and stock your book on their shelves. It's fine that you want to see your book in their store, but they don't want to see it unless it's selling.

In case bookstores don't see any sales, they want the ability to return the unsold stock and get a refund. That is revenue that comes out of your pocket if you allow for it. You'll see returns as an option that you can enable through IngramSpark. I recommend keeping the option disabled unless you have the funds to pay Ingram Book Group back for the returned copies.

IF YOU'RE GOING THE SELF-PUBLISHING ROUTE

In order to sell more books, you absolutely must produce the total package. This includes:

- Cover design
- Interior formatting
- Book descriptions (aka marketing copy)
- Reviews

These four items can make or break the success of your book. Authors who do not prioritize these areas will inevitably fail. If you're merely an author looking for a hobby, then by all means, don't place any importance here. Serious authors will put as much time and effort into these areas as they do into the writing and editing processes.

You'll find it no surprise that I recommend hiring out for three of the four items. The reason is that not just anyone can handle cover design and interior formatting effectively. It takes years of study and practice to deliver high-quality results at an elite level. Anything less than professional, and you're already working at a greater disadvantage.

It might take you hours, if not weeks or months, to create a passable cover design. What you may not know is that cover design is so much more than slapping on a cool graphic and some nifty fonts. Cover design is about the composition, color theme, trending genre-specific layouts, and so much more. What would take years for an amateur to create will take hours for an experienced professional.

Hiring an interior formatter isn't critical, but it'll certainly make for a better reading experience when you hire a professional who's well-versed in typesetting—the overall design of the text on each page. I've stumbled over countless indie authors who unknowingly format their interior improperly. The offenses range from left-aligning text—when it should be justified alignment—to cramming so much text on a page that the letters are nearly unreadable.

Can you format your interior for free? Absolutely, but you'll want to compare your interiors with other books within your niche. Skip right to the bestsellers lists for your answer. There's a reason they're ranking at the top. Chances are their total package has everything in place—the cover design, the interior formatting, the book description, and the reviews.

Draft2Digital, Reedsy, and even Google Docs are great for formatting interiors, so you don't even have to pull out your wallet. The interiors won't be quite as nice or flexible as premium software, but they can certainly give you a passable interior format. Should you have the money, invest in software like Vellum, Atticus, Scrivener, or my preference lately, Dibbly Create. These tools give you what you need and remove most of the guesswork out of formatting a book for digital and print fulfillment.

I'm often not patient enough to bother, so I prefer hiring out through places like Miblart, Fiverr, and Archangel Ink. Formatting rates vary wildly from one place to the other, with a rough range around $200 to $1500 or more.[v] It's worth it for me, because formatting can take hours to complete, especially if you're new to this business.

Once you have a killer cover and interior, you need to give browsing customers a reason to buy and read your book. That's where your book description comes into play. Unlike the text you wrote in your book, what you write for your book description is significantly different. View a good book description as marketing copy or a means to entice readers to buy your book. That's its sole purpose.

You're not trying to summarize what you cover within the book. Effective marketing copy should create enough intrigue to leave your potential readers clamoring to get their hands on your content. In *Mastering Amazon Descriptions*, indie author Brian Meeks shares some of the best practices for crafting marketing copy that converts book browsers to buyers. When I interviewed him multiple times, I learned that an interesting book description will have a few key elements:

1. A strong hook: Lead with your best stuff. Since you're a nonfiction author, you can lead with your potential reader's problem, then show how your book is their solution.
2. Concise, punchy sentences: Keep your writing at a fourth-grade reading level so that browsing customers can quickly and easily understand what your book is all about, even at a glance.
3. A "you'll love this because" statement: Toward the end of your description, tell them precisely why your book is the best option they've seen all day. Lead with a "love" statement, then close out with why. For example: "You'll love this comprehensive book on keywords, because it's easy to follow and will teach you what you need to forever master the subject."
4. Call-to-action: Keep it simple with a statement like, "Buy it now." Don't overcomplicate this part. If a browsing customer made it this far in your description, they only need a simple prompt to buy it now.

Brian's method isn't the only way to write a description. I'll leave a list of recommended reads in the Resources section should you want to learn more about better copywriting.

Until recently, authors had to rely on intuition and constant revisions to get it right. Or, sometimes, they hire a pro. I've leaned on a few services to handle book descriptions but have more recently found generative AI (artificial intelligence) to be very helpful.

All you have to do is present AI with all the facts about your book, including relevant keywords, and provide a sample book description so the machine knows how you'd like your copy to flow. From there, AI can create a decent book description. You'll need to do some editing so it's less dry and sounds more natural, but at least you'll have a place to start.

I love how I can take a collection of relevant keywords and have AI seamlessly weave them throughout the description. In the past, I would toil away for hours crafting the perfect description that used some keywords, but my efforts always came out forced and stilted.

Not with generative AI. Services like ChatGPT can generate a description and work with you on refining it. More recently, I started using Dibbly Create for writing my books and video content. The AI-assistant KIP has several features that work in tandem with the word processor. When you write within their system, KIP can analyze what you wrote and provide a detailed description. Again, it's not perfect, so you can expect to do a little editing and do a bit of back and forth with the AI.

However, that could be the difference between spending upwards of $150 on a book description or nothing when using AI. It's your choice, and you'll ultimately know how effective your ad copy is when you make sales. If you're actively driving traffic and still not getting sales, then chances are likely you'll need to update your cover or refine your book description.

How you drive that traffic comes down to your strategies for marketing and promotion. The hobbyist author will write, publish, and repeat with no effort placed on driving traffic and building awareness. The savvy business author will pour more effort into marketing and promotion than they ever did in producing the book.

That's the perfect segue into talking about the bane of some author's existence: marketing and promoting.

CHAPTER 9:
MARKETING AND PROMOTING YOUR BOOK

The key to reaching more readers and selling more books is marketing and promoting. Writing and publishing a book alone does not grant you the ability to inform the world of your presence through telepathy. What matters most are the efforts you put into being as visible as possible to your ideal reader.

Unlike writing a nonfiction book in twenty-four hours, marketing and promotion is a never-ending task you simply can't condense down to any one period, especially if you want to sell more books continuously.

Have you ever noticed how the largest companies and most famous brands continue to promote themselves through paid media placement like commercials, billboards, magazines and the like? Why would McDonald's need to tell people to come eat at their restaurants? Isn't McDonald's world-famous enough not to have to sink millions of dollars into ad campaigns? What about Nike? Why do they need athlete endorsements or visibility through sponsoring large sporting events?

These two massive corporations do it because they know business is about vying for the consumer's time and money. If consumers aren't thinking about you, your brand, or your product, then they'll be thinking about somebody else's brand, service, or product. When someone wants a quick bite to eat, they'll remember some random commercial they heard on the radio about McDonald's over Five Guys restaurants. Should someone need athletic footwear or clothes, that person will remember their favorite celebrity or athlete wearing the latest line of Nike shoes.

These companies could stop pouring millions of dollars into marketing and promoting their products, but they might lose the consumer's attention to other competing products. You're in that same fight to gain relevance in the consumer's minds. People need to make millions of instant decisions based on the data they receive from their surrounding environment. When they need a good read, they'll search it out. What are the books they'll be searching for? The ones recommended by friends, seen in commercials, noticed on local media appearances, or otherwise showcased memorably.

The primary goal of marketing and promoting your book and author brand comes down to being more consistently visible. Any opportunity you have to present your book to a potential new reader is the perfect chance to grow your brand.

Let's take a quick overhead view of potential avenues to get you and your book in front of more readers. The good news is you won't need a million-dollar budget—though that wouldn't hurt—to reach more readers and sell more books consistently.

Regardless of the advice I dispense, understand there is no silver bullet that'll solve all your marketing and promotional issues. Every author needs to explore what works best based on their resources, including time, money, and influence. The key to selling more books is discovering what works for you through experimentation and adapting your focus as needed.

As with anything, when you fail to plan, you plan to fail. I don't expect you to close the book after reading this chapter with a fully sorted-out plan. If you want something a bit more precise, consider checking out my four-time award-winning book, *Promotional Strategies for Books*. For now, I'll present you with a few broad strokes and a general understanding of what you need to get your book in front of more readers. As long as you create a book with a dialed-in package—great cover design, book description, interior formatting, and reader reviews—getting it in front of people is all you need to do right now. The book should sell itself if you have all the right items in place.

We already discussed the power of identifying your target audience or ideal reader, so you know how important it is to get your book in front of your audience where they're at. As you're developing your book, note where your readers congregate most and meet them there. While paid advertising through platforms like Amazon or Facebook yield pretty incredible results, sometimes the most effective marketing strategies are the ones that come free. Let's explore some of those low-cost alternatives and briefly touch on some premium options.

SOCIAL MEDIA & ONLINE PLATFORMS FOR BOOK PROMOTION

Oh, boy, I've opened up a highly polarizing topic. Many would-be experts believe that social media marketing is dead or that it's highly ineffective for direct sales of books. However, over the past few years, that's changed. Shopify and other platform-based shops like TikTok Shop or Instagram Shops allow you to present consumers with the best options with the least friction. Simply offering a shop or online retailer link, however, doesn't mean you will sell books.

Remember how I said the goal of marketing and promotion is to be as visible as possible? Well, where do you think millions of your ideal readers congregate most? On platforms like Facebook, X, Instagram, TikTok, and even YouTube, authors have plenty of options to choose from. Similar to promoting your book, simply setting up a social account isn't enough to get people to notice you.

In order for social media to be truly effective selling books, you must do what the name itself implies—be social! You must connect with one reader at a time by being the perfect ambassador for your books and brand.

Leveraging social media for book promotion doesn't mean you have to be constantly online and available on every platform. Stick with one social media platform and don't deviate from it. Find one site or service you enjoy which has some of your ideal audience eagerly awaiting. Regardless of how niche your subject, almost every platform will have a pocket of hyper-specific readers.

According to a report from April 2023,[vi] Facebook has nearly three billion active monthly users. Even if you write in the most random niche known to man, the odds are at least slightly in your favor when dipping into a pool of people that number in the billions. Imagine reaching only a fraction of that, like 1%. That's thirty million users.

Realistically, will you reach that many users? Probably not, but you certainly increase your odds of success by being a part of that crowd and engaging in meaningful ways. Before you hop onto Facebook and claim it as your territory, you need to come ready for the party.

Set up your social media profile in a way that showcases who you are and what you do. Load your profile with professional headshots, relevant links, and posts that further cement your reputation as the go-to expert in your field.

Your photo doesn't have to come from an extravagant Glamour Shots photo session, especially since you can take great photos with any of the latest mobile technology by Apple iOS or Android. Should you not have your hands on that type of technology, ask someone who has. I was fortunate to ask my sister-in-law for some headshots because of her extensive background in photography. She was kind enough to set me up with a professional photographer to do a photo shoot at no cost.

Granted, I was rather lucky to have that opportunity, but it only came from asking around. Prior to that, I took a simple picture or two with my phone, had it professionally cleaned up, then used it across all social media and for my book branding.

Use one image everywhere so your brand—your face—remains permanently etched in people's brains. I know you probably have a killer array of photos showcasing you from every imaginable angle, but you need to settle for just one and use that one consistently.

Next, you'll want to dial in your message so it's clean and clear. Arnold Schwarzenegger once asked, "Who is your daddy? And what does he do?" You need to express that in as few words as possible. Most social media profiles allow you to fill out a profile with a short bio; that's where you'll tell people who you are and what you do.

In every place you'll find me, my message is simple.

CHAPTER 9: MARKETING AND PROMOTING YOUR BOOK

> *I'm Dale L. Roberts. I teach authors how to write and publish books that sell.*

While that message might not work for you, it's an example of how direct you need to be.

When given the choice to share a link, I highly recommend using a catch-all link to redirect potential visitors to various aspects of your business. I prefer using the free version of Linktree, while others lean on premium services provided by other similar companies. One of the least effective uses of a link is simply entering your book link. What if a visitor already has your book? It's likely they won't use it. That wastes your one opportunity to steer them toward something that is relevant to them.

In my Linktree, I include all relevant publications, preferred resources, and recommended services, making it easy for anyone who visits my profile to know precisely where to find what they need to know. On your feed, include value-based posts that promote engagement. Creating posts doesn't mean you should promote the hell out of your book, though you can still do that in subtle ways.

For instance, if you're providing a tip about the best at-home workouts, you could lightly touch on your book.

> *"Have you tried any of these seven at-home workouts? If so, what do you find most effective for weight loss? In my bestselling book, The 90-Day Home Workout Plan, I showcased an exercise plan similar to at-home workout #5."*

You'd then either insert a link to the post you're referring to or direct visitors to visit your link in bio. If you post with enough consistency and substance, people on social media will come to rely on you for insights and information in your area of expertise.

I built my brand of self-publishing education by consistently showing up on one of the most used social media avenues: YouTube. Although I've made small strides on Facebook, Twitter, Instagram, and TikTok, YouTube has been the most powerful platform for my business.

Demonstrating value through video is the single most effective way for me to gain new followers and readers. I don't have to make my videos entirely about the books I publish since I can mention my book in subtle ways, like placing a link on my channel's landing page, in the video descriptions, and in the pinned comments. Not to mention that YouTube now offers a merch shelf to showcase my books through a Shopify integration.

Rather than sending traffic only to places like Amazon, I can get a direct sale, removing the middleman. I get a larger cut and keep my audience to myself. You can imagine a huge reason for me mentioning my presence on YouTube in my books is so people subscribe to me over there and stick around for the value-based content I provide. When it comes time for my next major book release, I can lean heavily on my platform to host a successful book launch.

While Facebook and YouTube are both great avenues, they aren't the only ones for you to consider, merely just examples of places you can build and grow your brand. In order to leverage social media to sell more books, you need to be present and social to make it all come together. The more you actively contribute within your community, the more you'll get in return. Goodwill goes a long way in the grand scheme of things.

COLLABORATIONS & PUBLICITY

Let's say you aren't all about that life of grinding it out while building a presence on social media. Quite a few influential people might work with you or promote your work for a small fee. I prefer collaborating with authors or brands with a similar-sized following, so no money ever has to exchange hands.

You get bonus points for working with other authors in your field, because you both stand to gain something out of a collaboration.

Working with other authors is rather simple. You can coordinate newsletter swaps where you promote their book to your email list while the other author returns the favor. Getting placement in front of your ideal audience this way doesn't cost a dime. All it requires is your willingness to meet and get to know other authors within your field.

When you grow a wide enough network, you can also consider group promos. A group promo works when multiple authors promote deeply discounted books on a specific date. Every author drops the price of their books, then promotes that deal to their followers—whether through social media or email marketing campaigns.

A couple of services to consider for arranging email newsletter swaps or group promos include StoryOrigin or BookFunnel. Rather than worrying about managing all the moving parts, these services act as a middle ground for authors of all types to work together. While I still recommend connecting directly with authors within your niche, these premium services remove the awkward ice-breaking conversation you'd normally have if you were arranging a collaboration. Through that goodwill, though, you should have ample reason to connect with the author beyond that single collaboration, especially if it's been mutually beneficial.

You're only limited by your imagination and willingness to break out of your shell and meet other authors in your space. Sometimes, you might even run into an influencer who's willing to work with you in some capacity. I'm always open to collaborations—both big and small—since I take no readers for granted.

What if you want to work with the biggest influencers with the widest reach? That becomes trickier and may require a significant investment.

Throw a stick and you'll find many paid influencer opportunities you can use to promote your book, but will they be effective? Is that money well spent? Do your research before investing a single dime into influencer marketing, because you want to work with someone who doesn't just have a large follower count. Instead, you want an influencer with an active following. It's better to work with an influencer with 1,000 raving and active fans than someone with a million followers and hardly any engagement.

Attention is social currency these days and the only way to capture that is through engagement. If no one is actively contributing to a post or an influencer's efforts, then it's a waste. I can't tell you the number of times I've heard of some poor author who threw a bunch of money into influencer marketing only to see zero sales.

Choose your paid marketing strategies wisely and investigate all your options before running with one. Referrals and word-of-mouth will be the most effective way of weeding out what may or may not work.

Marketing and promotions extend beyond just this one chapter. I'm always willing to try any one strategy for publicity once, especially if it doesn't require a financial investment. From guest blogging, podcast interviews, and speaking engagements to media coverage, you have many avenues to test and explore for publicity for your book and author brand. You just need to consistently promote and stay in front of your ideal audience in some capacity, no matter how big or small.

CONCLUSION: ACHIEVING YOUR NONFICTION WRITING GOALS IN LIMITED TIME

Writing a nonfiction book in twenty-four hours is much more than accomplishing an amazing feat. It's all about taking massive freaking action so you can focus more on the other details like editing, proofreading, formatting, marketing, and promoting. The consensus among experienced authors is that the first draft is just the beginning, and the real hurdles come afterward.

I've given you more than ample permission to write a bad first draft. In fact, I expect you to write a crappy first draft; it's nearly a requirement as an author. As long as you plan ahead, the process shouldn't be too difficult.

Choose a genre that best matches your interests and skill set. This removes any potential friction that will come from breaking into a genre you have no passion for or knowledge about. I've seen it happen far too often: A new author doesn't know what to write, so they go after the current shiny object or trend. Afterwards, they end up stuck with an asset they don't care for. Even worse, they haven't learned and don't comprehend what caused it to fail.

When times get tough and book sales are lean, what'll guide you through those times is the passion you have for your subject or interest. Having insights into a niche puts you at a greater advantage over folks who simply break into it for the sake of money. Getting paid for your efforts is essential, but make sure it doesn't come at the cost of your integrity or sanity.

While plugging into your passions, you'll want to gather relevant resources and information pertinent to your future publication. Having your research in order before you write makes putting pen to paper immensely easier when the time comes. I wouldn't ever recommend writing a book without having at least a tenuous grasp on your subject and a basic understanding of what is credible and worth sharing.

The single most important piece in writing a nonfiction book efficiently is the outline. While I applaud discovery writers for their willingness to improvise until they get a book done, that method will prove to be a bit more problematic when your window of time is merely one day. Some pantsers (another term for discovery writers) can get away with writing a book in twenty-four hours, but they are probably the exception to the rule.

pantser: A writer who creates stories without an outline, letting the plot unfold spontaneously as they write. They're known for writing by the seat of their pants.

That outline is going to be the road map that guides you to your ultimate destination of finishing your book in record time so you can then seamlessly transition to the next steps. It'd certainly be nice to write a first draft and publish it for the entire world to see, but as you'll remember, that isn't the case. Even the most practiced sculptor spends weeks, months, and sometimes years chiseling away at their work to produce the very best piece of art. You're no different, except you don't have to spend even remotely that long refining your work after the initial production.

Once your outline is all sorted out, try your hand at all three ways to write—touch-typing, voice dictating, and transcribing. Find the method most efficient for you. At first, you might have a deadlock among all three, but with practice, you'll get better. You just have to practice consistently to reap the rewards.

When producing this book, I started with voice dictation but transitioned to touch-typing when I realized I wasn't working nearly as fast as I would've liked to. If I had a longer window of time to finish my book, I'd have been willing to keep working on my voice dictation skills. Since I set my deadline at twenty-four hours, I needed what worked now instead of later. That's why I leaned into the old skill I picked up in high school, compliments of Mrs. Nagel.

Once you have that manuscript done, the work has only just begun. By expediting your first draft, you'll have more time to dedicate to essential elements like editing.

Outsourcing the editing process is what'll give you an edge over authors who try to do it all themselves. While authors may think their work is flawless, readers frequently point out the lack of editing as the reason for low ratings in reviews. Never skip at least three rounds of deep edits on your manuscript. This includes structural editing, copyediting, and proofreading.

A few of the other options—like beta reading, ARC readers, and producing an audiobook—aren't as essential, but could make a world of a difference. I wish I could realistically present a way to

CONCLUSION: ACHIEVING YOUR NONFICTION WRITING GOALS IN LIMITED TIME

edit your book in one day, but it's certainly not possible given that you probably don't have live-in editors at your home or office. The complexity of scheduling your edits with a professional is outside your control and unless you have the deep pockets of Jeff Bezos, money won't be enough of a motivating factor for an editor to drop everything they're doing to handle your manuscript.

It'll then take time for you to digest the editor's notes and make any necessary corrections. It is not possible to rush the editing process without sacrificing quality.

Once you fully edit your manuscript, it's ready to be formatted and made market-ready with a killer cover design, book description, interior formatting, and at least fifteen reviews or more on launch day.

After that, it's up to you to distribute your book into every imaginable avenue so you reach the most readers possible. Though some would have you believe Amazon is the be-all, end-all for authors, that's not entirely true. Quite a few authors are seeing massive success through other platforms like Draft2Digital, IngramSpark, Kobo Writing Life, and so on. Investigate every avenue to see what works best for you and your book.

I'd rather not have my book live and die on any one platform. That's why I embrace a wide publishing mindset in this business. Do I miss out on earnings I could otherwise get from exclusivity to platforms like Amazon? Possibly, but I don't want to miss that one opportunity I have to reach a reader who may not be on Amazon. Between online retailers, brick-and-mortar bookstores, and libraries, my book deserves to be showcased in as many places as possible. I don't go through all that effort to produce a book only for it to remain exclusive to one platform.

Even when you've chosen all the right avenues for publishing, getting more readers and book sales are entirely up to you. Authors are solely responsible for marketing and promotion, whether through free or premium options. The more consistently visible you can be, the better. Figure out some way to get yourself in front of more people every day. You are the single most effective advocate for your book, so you must get out from behind your keyboard and into the world, so more people know you and your book exist.

Now comes the single most important part of this entire book: taking the first step. While writing a nonfiction book isn't feasible for everyone, the information and details provided in this book are enough to help you work more efficiently and get your book done sooner rather than later. Then you can focus on the more labor-intensive items like marketing, promoting, or producing your next book. The more prolific you are, the more opportunities potential readers have to discover your author brand.

Should you fall short of writing a book in one day, don't lose heart. After working on this very book for the past twenty-three hours (with sleep added in there), I can confidently say it was a near failure. Would it have been the end of the world had I not finished? No, because I'd have a significant chunk of a book complete, so then all I'd have to do is wrap things up and move on to the next steps.

I expect you can do the same thing too, but it'll take time, practice, and patience. When you finally write a nonfiction book in twenty-four hours for the first time, it'll boost your confidence, save time, and build a legacy that'll echo for generations to come.

Good luck and never give up!

A SMALL ASK...

Now that you've finished reading this book, what do you think of what you read? Are there any tips or information you found insightful? What do you think is missing from this book? While you're thinking back on what you read, it'd mean the world to me if you left an honest review on Amazon.

As you probably know, reviews play a part in building relevancy for all products on Amazon. Whether or not you found the information helpful, your candid review will help other customers make an informed purchase.

Also, based on your review, I'll adjust this publication and future editions. That way, you and other indie authors can learn and grow.

Leave a review at DaleLinks.com/Review24Hours.

ABOUT THE AUTHOR

Dale L. Roberts is an award-winning author and video content creator. After publishing over fifty titles and becoming an international bestselling author on Amazon multiple times across various regions, Dale started his YouTube channel, Self-Publishing with Dale. After seven years of producing high-quality content about self-publishing, Dale has cemented his position as the go-to authority in the indie-author community.

Dale currently lives with his wife Kelli and two rescue cats in Columbus, Ohio.

Relevant links:

- My Books—DaleLinks.com/MyBooks
- Website—SelfPublishingWithDale.com
- YouTube—YouTube.com/SelfPublishingWithDale
- YouTube Podcast—YouTube.com/@SelfPubWithDale
- Discord—DaleLinks.com/Discord
- X (fka Twitter)—Twitter.com/SelfPubWithDale
- Facebook—Facebook.com/SelfPubWithDale
- Instagram—Instagram.com/SelfPubWithDale

SPECIAL THANKS

Jeanne De Vita and her tireless work editing my books. I cannot express enough gratitude for this beautiful human being. With every edit, she guides me to write better and clearer. If you're ever looking for the best editor to work on your nonfiction manuscript, you've gotta hire Jeanne. She's truly one of a kind!

And a big special thanks to all my community members on YouTube and Discord. You guys are the best!

RESOURCES

VIDEOS I RECOMMEND:

- Write a Book in 24 Hours...or Delete It?! - https://dalelinks.com/24hourchallenge
- *There's No Such Thing as Writer's Block* by Honoree Corder - https://dalelinks.com/writersblock
- *Finish the Damn Book* by Martin McConnell - https://dalelinks.com/finishthebook

BOOKS I RECOMMEND:

- *Amazon Keywords for Books* - https://dalelinks.com/keywordsbook
- *How to Write a Book in 48 Hours* - https://dalelinks.com/48hoursbook
- *The Self-Publisher's Legal Handbook* - https://dalelinks.com/helensedwick
- *The 30-Day Author Plan* by Kevin Tumlinson - https://dalelinks.com/30daybook
- *The Consummate Fitness Professional* by Dale L. Roberts - https://dalelinks.com/fitpro

RESOURCES

- *The Stretch Workout Plan* by Dale L. Roberts - https://dalelinks.com/stretch
- *The Amazon Self Publisher* by Dale L. Roberts – https://dalelinks.com/selfpubbook
- *Mastering Amazon Descriptions* by Brian Meeks - https://dalelinks.com/meeksbook
- *How to Write a Sizzling Synopsis* by Bryan Cohen - https://dalelinks.com/sizzling
- *Promotional Strategies for Books* by Dale L. Roberts – https://dalelinks.com/promobook

RESOURCES I RECOMMEND:

- Nick Thacker's *Dictation for Authors* - https://dalelinks.com/bookcareer
- Author Level Up – https://www.youtube.com/@authorlevelup
- Typing Speed Test - https://dalelinks.com/typetest

SOFTWARE & SERVICES I RECOMMEND:

- Audacity - https://www.audacityteam.org/
- Descript - https://dalelinks.com/descript
- Riverside.FM – https://DaleLinks.com/Riverside
- Rev - https://DaleLinks.com/Rev
- Fiverr – https://DaleLinks.com/Fiverr
- ProWritingAid – https://DaleLinks.com/ProWritingAid
- Dibbly Create - https://DaleLinks.com/DibblyCreate
- StoryOrigin – https://DaleLinks.com/StoryOrigin

- Linktree – https://linktr.ee/
- Book Genie (editing services by Jeanne De Vita) – Book-Genie.com
- Ava Fails (book editing & more) – HeyYoAva.com

PLACES TO SELF-PUBLISH YOUR BOOK

- Draft2Digital – https://DaleLinks.com/D2D
- Amazon Kindle Direct Publishing (KDP) – https://kdp.amazon.com
- IngramSpark – https://www.ingramspark.com
- Kobo Writing Life – https://www.kobowritinglife.com
- Apple Books for Authors – https://authors.apple.com/
- Barnes & Noble Press – https://press.barnesandnoble.com/
- Google Play Books Partner Center – https://play.google.com/books/publish/u/0/
- PublishDrive – https://DaleLinks.com/PublishDrive
- Streetlib – https://www.streetlib.com
- BookBaby – https://DaleLinks.com/Bookbaby
- Laterpress – https://www.laterpress.com

REFERENCES

i U.S. Copyright Office. (2023 November 1). U.S. Copyright Office Fair Use Index. https://www.copyright.gov/fair-use/

ii Rutkowska, A. (2023 May 22). Book Launch Reviews: Launching with 100+ reviews. https://kindlepreneur.com/book-launch-reviews-launching-with-100-reviews/

iii Reedsy Ltd. (2023 Nov. 7). How to Set Your Freelance Editing Rates. https://blog.reedsy.com/freelancer/how-to-set-your-freelance-editing-rates/

iv Herbert, J. (2022 Aug. 15). Self-Publishing Versus Traditional Publishing: Pros And Cons For Leaders To Consider. https://www.forbes.com/sites/forbesbusinesscouncil/2022/08/15/self-publishing-versus-traditional-publishing-pros-and-cons-for-leaders-to-consider/?sh=7d7cd6486241

v Friedman, J. (2013 Apr. 24). How Much Attention Should You Pay to Book Design? A Q&A With Joel Friedlander. https://janefriedman.com/book-design-joel-friedlander-2/

vi Kemp, S. (2023 May 11). FACEBOOK USERS, STATS, DATA & TRENDS. https://datareportal.com/essential-facebook-stats

www.ingramcontent.com/pod-product-compliance
Lightning Source LLC
Chambersburg PA
CBHW071722020426
42333CB00017B/2356